Workforce Housing
Innovative Strategies and Best Practices

Urban Land Institute

Fannie Mae Foundation

Homes *for* Working Families

About This Book

This *Workforce Housing: Innovative Strategies and Best Practices* book was sponsored and financed by the Fannie Mae Foundation and is the first publication in a series to be published by Homes for Working Families, a newly created 501c3 organization with the mission of demonstrating that the affordable housing crisis facing America is solvable and that solutions are available to concerned and committed communities.

Workforce Housing: Innovative Strategies and Best Practices looks at four programs and 11 projects that demonstrate creative solutions to the affordable housing crisis. The principles and best practices are drawn from an analysis of the programs and projects.

The Urban Land Institute is proud once again to have partnered with the Fannie Mae Foundation on this important effort and wishes Homes for Working Families success in this important mission of demonstrating that the affordable housing crisis in America is a problem that can be solved. Through this book and continuing research, we hope to support that mission by highlighting affordable housing success stories.

Richard M. Rosan
President

Recommended bibliographic listing:

ULI–the Urban Land Institute. *Workforce Housing: Innovative Strategies and Best Practices.* Washington, D.C.: ULI–the Urban Land Institute, 2006.

ULI Catalog Number: F19

ISBN: 978-0-87420-960-0

Copyright 2006 by ULI–the Urban Land Institute

1025 Thomas Jefferson Street, N.W.
Suite 500 West
Washington, D.C. 20007-5201

ULI Project Staff

Rachelle L. Levitt
Executive Vice President, Policy and Practice

Gayle Berens
Senior Vice President, Real Estate Practice

Richard Haughey
Director, Multifamily Development
Project Manager
Primary Author, Introduction

Alex Bond
ULI Scholar-in-Residence
Primary Author, Case Studies

Jennifer LeFurgy
Metropolitan Institute at Virginia Tech
Contibuting Author, Case Studies

Deborah L. Myerson
Deborah L. Myerson, LLC
Contibuting Author, Case Studies

Adam Ploetz
Planning Consultant
Contributing Author, Case Studies

Nancy H. Stewart
Director, Book Program
Managing Editor

Lori Hatcher
Marketing Director

David James Rose
Manuscript Editor, Case Studies

Betsy VanBuskirk
Art Director

Anne Morgan
Graphic Designer

Craig Chapman
Director, Production

Cover Images: Top: Old Town Square, Chicago, Illinois; courtesy of the Chicago Housing Authority.
Bottom: University Glen, Camarillo; California State University–Channel Islands.

About ULI–the Urban Land Institute

ULI–the Urban Land Institute is a nonprofit education and research institute that is supported by its members. Its mission is to provide responsible leadership in the use of land to enhance the total environment. ULI sponsors education programs and forums to encourage an open, international exchange of ideas and sharing of experiences; initiates research that anticipates emerging land use trends and issues and proposes creative solutions based on that research; documents best practices; provides advisory services; and publishes a wide variety of materials to disseminate information on land use and development. Established in 1936, ULI has more than 32,000 members in 80 countries representing the entire spectrum of the land use and development disciplines.

Richard M. Rosan
President

About Homes for Working Families

Homes for Working Families seeks to increase the availability of high-quality homes within reach of America's working families by changing public opinion and public policy. We are working to create a consensus that moves the public to care, moves the issue of homes for working families to the forefront of our nation's domestic policy priorities, and moves policy makers to act. Our effort focuses on working families—the families of teachers, firefighters, retail clerks, librarians, and others who struggle to find homes they can buy or rent in the communities they serve.

Together with a diverse coalition of partners, we communicate the severe shortage of homes within reach of working families and the effect this problem has on everyone, spotlight policies and programs that help meet this need, and promote the understanding that these homes add vitality to local economies, improve the quality of life in communities, and bring stability to families.

Beverly L. Barnes
Executive Director

About the Fannie Mae Foundation

The Fannie Mae Foundation creates affordable home-ownership and housing opportunities through innovative partnerships and initiatives that build healthy, vibrant communities across the United States. The foundation is specially committed to improving the quality of life for the people of its hometown, Washington, D.C., and to enhancing the livability of the city's neighborhoods.

Stacey D. Stewart
President and CEO

Contents

Workforce Housing

Innovative Strategies and
Best Practices

Overview

The United States is the best housed nation in the world. In 2004, its homeownership rate soared to a record high—69 percent—and homeowners are now sitting on more than $10 *trillion* of home equity. This rising tide of household wealth fuels consumer spending: More people than ever before are tapping into their equity to finance their children's education, a secure retirement, an exotic vacation, a luxury car.

For most American homeowners, this is the best of times.

The same dynamic that is bringing so much wealth to so many is depriving many others of opportunity. The red-hot appreciation of housing prices has moved the dream of homeownership beyond the reach of many working families. Among low- to moderate-income families with children, the homeownership rate stands at 56 percent— a full percentage point below its rate a quarter of a century ago. The National Housing Conference reports that America's elementary school teachers, police officers, licensed practical nurses, retail salespersons, and janitors no longer qualify for a mortgage on a median-priced home. While a dramatic increase in subprime lending has allowed some working familes to achieve the dream of homeownership, it may also bring an increase in predatory lending practices. Unsuspecting families may be subject to excessive fees, prepayment penalties, loss of home equity, and, in the worst case, loss of their homes.

For America's working families, this is not the best of times.

The rental market offers no relief. Nowhere in the country today can a minimum-wage earner afford a two-bedroom apartment. More than 12 percent of American families are spending more than half their income on housing. One of every three families spends more than 30 percent of its income on housing. These figures do not include the 2.5 million families who live in crowded or structurally defective housing units. If, as is expected, long-term interest rates rise, more working families will be excluded from the homebuying market. This development would result in lower vacancy rates (and higher rental rates) for apartments, thereby increasing the burden on families already strained by housing costs.

As these trends have unfolded, and as the federal role in affordable housing policy has diminished, state and local governments have been forced to become ever more creative and flexible in their attempts to address the nation's shortage of affordable homes. But what is remarkable— *they are succeeding.*

This book looks at 15 of these success stories, providing overviews of states and localities that are demonstrating resiliency and adaptability in meeting the affordable homes challenge. Fifteen snapshot case studies provide a portrait of the progress that is possible when enlightened public policy is joined with innovative partnerships and creative problem solving.

Analysis of the case studies yields a set of underlying principles that may serve to guide states and localities that are grappling with the home affordability crisis. Many of these principles represent new ways of looking at this seemingly intractable problem. They suggest the need for a departure from orthodoxy, a break from past practices. In brief, these principles, outlined below, suggest that increasing the supply of homes within reach of working families demands a willingness to experiment.

Following are key principles of successful programs to develop homes within the financial reach of working families.

■ BEING FLEXIBLE, ADAPTABLE, COMPREHENSIVE

Montgomery County, Maryland, widely credited with having one of the nation's most effective affordable homes programs, displays an uncommon ability to adapt to changing market and regulatory realities. The county's moderately priced dwelling unit (MPDU) law has been modified more than 20 times since 1976. But the MPDU program is just one weapon in the full arsenal that the county's Housing Opportunity Commission (HOC) uses to increase the supply of homes available to low- and moderate-income families. The Montgomery County HOC combines programmatic flexibility with the understanding that no single program by itself can solve the problem of affordability.

■ USING PUBLIC RESOURCES TO PRIME THE PRIVATE PUMP

The city of *Denver* is home to the country's largest urban infill development, a 7.5-square-mile site that soon will include 800 affordable homes for sale and 800 affordable homes for rent. Making possible this development is the partnership between the city and a private developer in which the city provides reduced land costs, tax incentives, and creative financing.

In California, the *Santa Clara Unified School District* donated more than two acres of land to a local developer in exchange for a commitment to create 40 rental homes within the reach of teachers. California's Certificate of Participation (COP) program, traditionally used for school capital improvement projects, provided the financing.

■ TAPPING THE POWER OF PUBLIC/PRIVATE PARTNERSHIPS

First Ward Place in *Charlotte, North Carolina*, is an award-winning, mixed-income community jointly developed by the Charlotte Housing Authority (CHA) and the Bank of America CDC. The two organizations formed a complementary relationship: CHA secured federal HOPE VI funds and Bank of America qualified for low-income housing tax credits.

■ TAMING THE BUREAUCRACY

Many local governments now understand that extensive and expensive public review processes discourage new development. Expediting these processes—and waiving fees for developers of homes that working families can afford—often jump-starts development. In *Austin, Texas*, the S.M.A.R.T. Housing Initiative offers developers three benefits: development fee waivers, expedited review by S.M.A.R.T. staff, and troubleshooting assistance with the development approval processes by S.M.A.R.T. staff trained to break logjams.

In *Massachusetts*, the Comprehensive Permit Law provides developers of homes within reach of working families a streamlined approval process that cuts through local roadblocks.

■ MIXING IT UP

The negative image of affordable housing, the residue of the high-density public housing projects of decades past, continues to feed community opposition to affordable home developments. Mixed-income developments, notable both for their attractiveness and their financial feasibility, counter these outdated images and often nullify opposition. In *Fairfax County, Virginia*, the Affordable Dwelling Unit Ordinance encourages mixed-income development by providing for a sliding scale of affordability.

A similar sliding scale accounts for the success of Murphy Park in *St. Louis*, once a crime-ridden public housing project that has been reinvented as a mixed-income community that includes both apartments and townhomes.

■ GIVING NEW MEANING TO HOME ECONOMICS

A community that provides a mix of homes to buy and homes to rent encourages renters to aspire to become homeowners. This is especially true if the community provides homebuyer education or financial literacy programs. Families renting a home in First Ward Place in Charlotte, North Carolina, are required to participate in the Charlotte Housing Authority's Family Self-Sufficiency Program, which prepares families for the challenges of homeownership. Credit repair and budgeting basics are among the topics taught.

A similar "home economics" program is underway in the Noji Gardens mixed-income development in *Seattle, Washington*.

■ RESPECTING SMART GROWTH, GREEN, AND TRANSIT-ORIENTED DEVELOPMENT PRINCIPLES

Generating public support for developments of homes within reach of working families begins with respecting public sentiment. Developments that are consistent with smart growth, in accordance with green building standards, and near mass transit are easier for officeholders and the public to support. In *San Jose, California*, the local transit agency and a private developer created new homes within reach of working families on the former parking lot of a transit station. The Ohlone-Chynoweth development, home to a demographic group that relies heavily on mass transit, rewards the public's investment in the transit system by providing built-in ridership.

■ CONNECTING THE DOTS BETWEEN HOMES WITHIN REACH AND ECONOMIC VITALITY

When home prices get higher, commutes become longer and employees become both less satisfied and (over time) less productive. Employers understand this dynamic—the connection between home availability and employee productivity. And what employers have long known, community leaders are now learning.

The Casa del Maestro development came into existence because *Santa Clara, California*, teachers could not afford to live in Santa Clara. Retaining good teachers became difficult. Attracting new teachers became more difficult. The plight of teachers became emblematic of Santa Clara's larger employee-retention, employee-recruitment problems. Understanding the potential economic impact, private businesses have donated millions of dollars to fund homes that working families can afford.

The Carrington development in *Fairfax County, Virginia*, grew out of the recognition that Fairfax teachers, nurses, police officers, firefighters, and county employees could not afford to live in the counties they served.

In *Camarillo, California*, home prices were making it tough for California State University–Channel Islands to recruit faculty and staff. Through the innovative use of vacant land, the university developed market-rate apartments to support an inventive program that enables faculty and staff to buy homes they can afford on campus.

In *Marshall, Minnesota*, the town's major employer—Schwan's Food—provided construction loans and funds for the development of 128 homes within reach that will be occupied by its employees and their families.

■ DESIGNING AS DISGUISE

Good design has never been more important. If the public is to support the development of homes close to the jobs of working families, these homes must fit seamlessly into existing communities. This aesthetic requirement, of course, clashes with the density dictated by financial considerations. But creative architects are welcoming this challenge, disguising density through the strategic use of open space and quadruplex configurations. In *Fairfax, Virginia*, the Edgemoore at Carrington development consists primarily of $1 million luxury homes. The developer was required to bring into this setting eight townhomes selling for $120,000 each. The city's "Great House" design effort made possible this integration. The eight units were constructed to look like two mansions, which blended seamlessly with the surrounding luxury homes.

In conclusion, no set of guiding principles—no rules of the road —can ensure the availability of more homes that are within reach of working families. The principles outlined in this executive summary do not define one precise route to success. Rather, they tell us that different communities are taking *different* routes to success. They tell us that *success is possible.* Throughout the country, success stories are multiplying. By featuring these stories, the Fannie Mae Foundation, the Urban Land Institute, and Homes for Working Families aim to inspire more efforts to find more solutions to the challenge of giving more working families greater opportunity to live in safe, decent homes in safe, decent communities.

Matrix of Programs and Developments

The matrix presented here offers a schematic overview of the case studies covered in this executive summary. It attests to the range of local and state activities now focused on the affordability challenge. It points to the need for flexibility and openness, for innovation and experimentation. It reminds us that the challenge of providing homes within the financial reach of working families is a moving target and that solutions must be tailored to ever-changing demographic, political, and market realities.

Programs	Locations	Highlights
S.M.A.R.T. Housing Initiative	Austin, Texas	• Self-funding due to increased tax base • Expedited permit review and fee waivers • Sliding scale of affordability requirements • Promotes transit-oriented and green development
The Housing Trust of Santa Clara	Santa Clara, California	• Mostly privately funded • Includes homebuyer assistance and counseling • Provides low-interest loans to multifamily developers • Connects affordable housing and economic development
Moderately Priced Dwelling Unit Program	Montgomery County, Maryland	• One of the country's most effective inclusionary zoning programs • Requires percentage of all new home developments to be affordable • Disperses affordable homes throughout the county • Includes homebuyer education and counseling
Chapter 40B—the Comprehensive Permit Law	Commonwealth of Massachusetts	• Statewide affordable homes law • Allows developers to override local development regulations for affordable home developments • Discourages exclusionary zoning practices • Stresses importance of affordable homes to economic health of state

Programs	Locations	Highlights
Stapleton	Denver, Colorado	• Tax increment financing • Innovative land acquisition strategy • Close relationship with local public school representatives • Low-income housing tax credits
Casa del Maestro	Santa Clara, California	• Partnership between for-profit developer and local school district • Surplus school property used for development • Affordable homes used as recruitment and retention technique for public school teachers • Prototype for other school districts and other occupations, such as police and firefighters
Edgemoore at Carrington	McLean, Virginia	• Inclusionary zoning • Density bonus in exchange for affordability • "Great House" design incorporates townhomes into luxury single-family detached community
Noji Gardens	Seattle, Washington	• Modular construction to reduce overall construction costs • Tax abatements • Mixed-income community • Homebuyer education and counseling
Ohlone-Chynoweth Commons	San Jose, California	• Transit-oriented development • Low-income housing tax credits • Federal Transit Administration grant • Expedited application review
Marshall Parkway	Marshall, Minnesota	• Employer-assisted homes • Homebuyer education, counseling, and downpayment assistance • Tax increment financing • USDA rural development loans

Programs	Locations	Highlights
University Glen at California State University–Channel Islands	Camarillo, California	• Affordable homes for sale to university faculty and staff • Leased land • Tax-exempt bonds • Innovative self-funding financing, whereby market-rate apartments and retail fund affordable units
Murphy Park	St. Louis, Missouri	• Low-income housing tax credits • Rehabilitation of public schools through partnership of developer and local schools • Significant infrastructure improvements • Mixed-income community replacing failed public housing project
First Ward Place	Charlotte, North Carolina	• HOPE VI grants • Public/private partnership • Mixed-income community replacing failed public housing project • Homebuyer education and counseling
New Pennley Place	Pittsburgh, Pennsylvania	• AFL-CIO assistance • HOPE VI grants • Renovation of existing buildings combined with new construction • Mixed-income community replacing failed public housing project • Significant city infrastructure improvements
Cabrini-Green/Near North Initiative	Chicago, Illinois	• Public/private partnership • HOPE VI funds • Tax increment financing • Mixed-income community replacing failed public housing project

Introduction:

Principles of Successful Affordable Housing Programs and Developments

Almost 70 percent of American families now own their own home and home prices have increased in all 163 markets tracked by Freddie Mac's conventional home mortgage price index.[1] More people than ever are participating in and benefiting from the realization of the "American dream." For many, this has created wealth in the form of home equity, which has been tapped to improve their quality of life through home improvements, new cars, and family vacations.

The red-hot appreciation of housing prices in many markets, however, has moved the dream of homeownership beyond the reach of many low- and moderate-income households and has created significant hardships for struggling families. In many cities, housing price appreciation has far exceeded gains in income. And while rents have dropped in some markets due to the exodus of renters taking advantage of historically low interest rates, many of those left renting are spending a large percentage of their income for housing. While a dramatic increase in subprime lending has allowed some working families to achieve the dream of homeownership, it may also bring an increase in predatory lending practices. Unsuspecting families are subject to excessive fees, prepayment penalties, loss of home equity, and, in the worst case, loss of their homes.[2]

In 2001, the most recent year for which data are available, 14.4 million American families or one in seven households paid more than half their household's income for housing and/or lived in substandard conditions.[3] While the worst housing problems are overwhelmingly concentrated among those at the bottom of the income distribution, the number of middle-quintile households (earning $32,000 to $50,000) who spent 30 percent or more of their incomes on housing jumped from 3.2 million in 1997 to 4.5 million in 2001.[4] A study by the National Housing Conference reports that America's elementary school teachers, police officers, licensed practical nurses, retail salespersons, and janitors would not qualify to purchase a median-priced home based on median income in most American cities.[5] In cities with hot real estate markets, even many two-wage-earning families spend more than 30 percent of their combined salaries on rent. The Fannie Mae Foundation further reports that after years of steadily declining, the incidence of crowding, defined as 1 to 1.5 persons per room, is once again on the rise.[6]

Any future increase in long-term interest rates may freeze many working families out of the homebuying market, which will lower the vacancy rates of rental apartments, leading to inevitable increases in rent taking a bigger chunk out of the paychecks of the lowest-income households. While some markets may see home prices decline, many economists believe the more likely scenario in most markets will be stabilizing home prices, which, when combined with rising interest rates, will keep homeownership unattainable for many.

With the prospect of continuing serious housing affordability problems in most major metropolitan areas and a continuing decentralization of housing policy to the states and municipalities, providing housing that is affordable to low- and moderate-income households has become increasingly challenging. State and local governments with limited resources and increasingly stressed affordable housing developers have been forced to become ever more creative and flexible in their attempts to address this intractable problem.

In this book, we take a look at how several state and local agencies and affordable housing developers have adapted to the increasingly constrained environment of affordable housing production. The case studies highlight numerous successful affordable housing developments and several outstanding public programs that have worked to provide much-needed affordable housing. Certain themes and principles emerge from the case studies that provide guidance to state and local governmental agencies and to affordable housing developers as they attempt to solve this crisis. Many of these principles represent a way of looking at the problem that is profoundly different from the way we looked at it in the past.

Take a comprehensive and flexible approach to affordable housing policies and programs.

In the current political and fiscal environment, there is no silver bullet to solve this problem. The most successful communities use numerous tools and constantly adjust to changing market realities. Montgomery County, Maryland, is widely credited with having an effective affordable housing program. Its Moderately Priced Dwelling Unit (MPDU) program is held up as a model throughout the country, yet it is only one component of the county's efforts. The Housing Opportunities Commission (HOC) administers the program along with below-market-rate loans for homebuyers and a portfolio of public housing scattered throughout the county to rent to low- and moderate-income families. In addition, the planning department plans for affordability by planning for higher-density housing in appropriate areas. It is important to note that since its enactment in 1976, the MPDU law has been modified more than 20 times, speaking to the need for flexibility in affordable housing regulations. Since the success of the MPDU law is tied to continuing growth in the county, which is facing build-out, leaders are again adjusting to the new market realities, making smaller infill developments subject to the law. The forces that have created the affordable housing problem are numerous, interrelated, and complex. A comprehensive approach to addressing the many levels of the problem is required. Having the flexibility to adjust to changing market and regulatory realities is the key to an ongoing successful affordable housing production program.

Use public policies, programs, land, and money to leverage private investment in affordable housing.

While the federal role in the production of affordable housing continues to diminish, state and local governments are left to address the issue. With their limited resources, creativity is required. The most creative among them have been able to leverage significant private investment through public policy and the strategic use of public funds and lands.

City leaders in Denver saw an opportunity to address several public needs through the redevelopment of the former Stapleton airport site. With over seven square miles of land available, the redevelopment project is the largest urban infill development in the country. Through a public/private partnership, the city and a private developer are creating a mixed-use, sustainable master-planned community with 10 percent of the housing designated as workforce housing, which is housing for moderate-income working households. Through the use of tax increment financing, reduced land costs, and creative financing, 800 affordable for-sale and 800 affordable rental units will be constructed by private developers. By investing in infrastructure, local governments can make the production of affordable housing feasible.

Communities with smaller parcels of land are still able to leverage private development through the creative use of various tools. The Santa Clara Unified School District in Santa Clara, California, worked with a private developer to create 40 affordable rental apartments by donating 2.16 acres of surplus school land. To finance the project, the school district used California's Certificate of Participation (COP) program, which is generally used for school capital improvements projects. The district successfully argued that in Santa Clara, a high-cost area, housing for teachers was as important as a new gymnasium. The COP program allowed for funds to be tapped relatively quickly compared to alternative financing, allowing the district to bring the attractive development in under budget and on time.

Cities like Charlotte, Chicago, and St. Louis have brought private developers in to redevelop existing public housing sites. By taking land costs out of the pro forma; using federal, state, and local financing; and adding market-rate and workforce housing to the communities, they are able to make private development of affordable housing feasible, provide housing for a wide range of incomes and create new communities rather than "projects."

When appropriate, create public/private partnerships to develop affordable housing.

In an effective public/private partnership, each partner provides complementary skills. These partnerships can provide for new funding opportunities not available to each individual partner. They can often help with the entitlement process by bringing local knowledge and political connections to the process.

The variety of possible combinations is wide, depending on the needs of the development. Several of the case studies featured in this book were the result of successful public/private partnerships. First Ward Place, located in Charlotte, North Carolina, is an award-winning mixed-income community on the site of a former distressed public housing site. The Charlotte Housing Authority (CHA) initially engaged the NationsBank Community Development Corporation (now Bank of America Community Development Corporation) in Charlotte to serve as a development consultant. Seeing the advantages that could be created by partnering, the two jointly developed the project. NationsBank was able to secure low-income housing tax credits and the CHA assisted in securing federal HOPE VI funds. The CHA continues to own the land while the buildings are owned by First Ward Place LLC, of which NationsBank and the CHA are board members.

Potential problems that could emerge in public/private partnerships include political instability of public staff, differing priorities of partners, competing neighborhood interests, and multiple intermediaries. An effective partner provides skills or resources lacking in the other organization. The purpose, roles, and leadership of the partnership should be clearly defined to ensure a smooth partnership.

Make it easier to develop affordable housing by waiving fees, and expediting the entitlement and permitting process.

With dwindling resources, local government leaders are constantly trying to improve the efficiency of the delivery of public services. Some have realized that the extensive and expensive public review process for new development actually discourages new development. This is particularly true for affordable housing developments, which usually have much less financial flexibility, due to the restricted rents and sales prices of housing units and added community opposition. While the public review and permitting process addresses important issues of public health, safety, and welfare, it often is duplicative, arbitrary, and inefficient.

By expediting the review process for affordable housing development projects, local governments are supporting a much-needed public service without laying out significant public resources. While fee waivers do reduce public revenues, they represent a more politically palatable public expense than a direct public subsidy. The general public tends to view fee waivers, tax cuts, and abatements as a reduction in revenue rather than an expenditure of their tax dollars, making them—for many residents—a more acceptable way of funding public needs.

The city of Austin, Texas, has done a particularly good job of supporting high-quality development that is consistent with the city's stated goals, including affordable housing through its S.M.A.R.T. Housing Initiative. Housing built under this program is intended to be Safe, Mixed-income, Accessible, Reasonably priced, and Transit accessible, thus the S.M.A.R.T. acronym. Development that qualifies is eligible for three basic benefits—development fee waivers, expedited review by designated S.M.A.R.T. staff, and troubleshooting assistance with development approval processes by staff designated to break logjams. Fee waivers are granted on a sliding scale depending on the amount of affordable housing provided.

Assistance with the public approval process is also central to the Massachusetts Comprehensive Permit Law, which allows qualified affordable housing developments to go through an alternative streamlined approval process, removing local roadblocks. While expediting review and waiving fees make not be decisive in the ultimate financial feasibility of a project, it does provide savings of time, money, and frustration, making the difficult endeavor of developing affordable housing a little easier. As important, it clearly states to residents and government staff that affordable housing is a community priority and should truly be treated as such.

Support and build mixed-income communities, including market-rate units, when possible.

The failed urban high-density public housing projects of the past did damage to the perception of affordable housing that still reverberates today, decades later. The negative images of problems created by the concentration of poverty have been seared into the collective consciousness of much of the American public and tied to the term "affordable housing." Despite the fact that the new face of affordable housing includes beautiful mixed-income communities with affordable units indistinguishable from market-rate units, the vestigial memories of failed public housing towers continue to feed community opposition.

While there are a variety of social, financial, and political reasons why mixed-income communities are currently favored over development that concentrates the lowest-income households in one location, less community opposition to mixed-income communities is becoming an increasingly important reason as it is becoming more and more difficult to build anything anywhere. Increasing traffic congestion and school overcrowding have made community opposition to any new development standard in most urban areas. That opposition is often amplified for new development with an affordable housing component, due to community fears. This opposition comes despite the fact that most communities have an enormous housing affordability problem. Nurses,

teachers, firefighters, and police officers often cannot afford to live in the communities they serve. In many communities where the children of residents cannot afford to live, the residents will oppose housing that would allow their own children to live nearby. This new reality of current community opposition cannot be discounted and should be factored into any affordable housing development planning. Also required is a public relations campaign to educate the public on the new realities of affordable housing and its importance to their local economies.

Providing housing options for all income groups affords lower-income households access to the services and positive lifestyle benefits afforded to middle- and upper-income households. These communities provide opportunities for households to move up without moving out of their communities. Such developments are often more financially feasible to construct because the market-rate and workforce housing units can subsidize the units reserved for low-income households. Oftentimes, new mixed-income developments are easier to build political support for and get through the entitlement process than exclusively low-income housing.

The case studies presented in this book demonstrate a growing concern for workforce housing and providing housing for a mix of incomes. Incoporating flexibility into the mix of housing permits communities to address a variety of community housing needs and allows developers to build a variety of products, diversifying risk and making projects more financially feasible.

The concept of allowing a sliding scale of affordability runs throughout the case studies in this book. The Affordable Dwelling Unit Ordinance in Fairfax County, Virginia, makes such flexibility possible. The Edgemoore at Carrington development in McLean, Virginia, was subject to the ordinance and was permitted to provide moderate-income housing units rather than strictly low-income units. Permitting housing to be provided on a sliding scale of affordability allows the county to target different types of housing for different developments and communities as the specific situation warrants.

The Murphy Park community in St. Louis has been reinvented as a mixed-use community that includes public housing apartments as well as townhomes for upper-middle-income households. Formerly a crime-ridden public housing project, the community now thrives with the reopening and improvement of Jefferson Elementary School, now the best elementary school in the school district. Mixing housing choices within a community also allows for the economic success of its residents and provides incentives to move out of subsidized units.

Provide opportunities for affordable homeownership and provide homebuyer education.

In addition to providing housing for a mix of incomes, many new developments are providing a mix of rental and for-sale units. Along with providing the opportunity for renters to become homebuyers, adding for-sale units often adds to the stability, pride, and sense of community of a neighborhood.

Providing for-sale units, however, creates a host of issues to be addressed. Since the homebuyer is purchasing the home at a reduced price, resale of the property is usually controlled. Most are not permitted to resell for a specified period of time. Most sales also require the buyer to share the accumulated appreciation upon sale of the property, with the proceeds used to support additional affordable housing opportunities.

A common theme that runs through the case studies with for-sale units is that additional programs are required to support first-time homebuyers. Many such developments offer downpayment assistance or low-interest loans to first-time homebuyers. Homebuyer education programs are also important and offered by most developers.

Each family living in public housing units at First Ward Place in Charlotte are required to participate in the Charlotte Housing Authority's Family Self-Sufficiency (FSS) Program. The program helps individuals and families become financially independent and transition out of public housing in the mandatory five years. An integral part of the program is the Homeownership Institute, which teaches the responsibilities of homeownership, credit repair, and budgeting. Graduation from the institute is required to qualify for either the market-rate rentals or the for-sale units.

Noji Gardens in Seattle is a mixed-income development with for-sale and rental housing. The developer of the project sees homeownership education as a win for both the participant and the developer. Participants are better equipped to buy a home and developers create a client base of informed and willing homebuyers less likely to default on their mortgage.

Develop affordable housing that is consistent with smart growth, green building standards, and transit-oriented development principles.

In the current climate, getting affordable housing developments through the entitlement process can be a difficult proposition to say the least. Developers of affordable housing can often engender more community support and make the entitlement process easier not only by providing housing for a mix of incomes, but also by meeting other community needs.

Developments that are consistent with smart growth, that are developed in accordance with green building standards[7] including increased energy efficiency, and that provide access to mass transit not only provide a better quality of life for new and existing residents, but also are easier for politicians and neighbors to support. They often also have local advocacy groups that can be instrumental in building community support and getting necessary governmental approvals. Coalitions of supporters can prove crucial to the ultimate success of the project. In addition, rental developments with long-term affordability requirements can reduce property management costs through high-quality sustainable building practices.

In San Jose, California, the local transit agency and a private developer created new affordable housing on the former parking lot of a transit station. The Ohlone-Chynoweth development maximizes the existing public investment in the transit system while providing built-in ridership and convenient access for a demographic group that tends more than others to rely on mass transit.

All developers in the Stapleton redevelopment are required to build to the standards of the Home Builders Association of Metro Denver for energy efficiency, healthy indoor air, reduced water usage, and preservation of natural resources. In Austin, to qualify for the city's S.M.A.R.T. program, mentioned earlier, proposed developments must meet green building standards and be accessible to transit.

Make the connection between affordable housing and a community's economic health and economic development strategy.

There is a growing understanding among community leaders, especially in very expensive urban markets, that providing housing opportunities for all workers is an important part of the economic health of the community and the region. When workers have to commute long distances to work, and spend more time stuck in traffic, productivity falls because they spend less time at work.[8] In areas where affordable rental or for-sale homes are out of the reach of most workers, some will leave the area entirely seeking more affordable housing in other regions of the country, leaving labor shortages in their wake. While most companies have employees who span the income spectrum, from high-paid executives to lower-paid administrative staff, very few communities offer housing choices for households with the same variety of incomes, leaving many to commute long distances to work.

Several of the successful housing programs and developments highlighted here have been successful because community leaders have made the connection between affordable housing and a healthy economy and have translated that into political support for regulations that support affordable housing and affordable housing developments.

The Casa del Maestro development in Santa Clara, California, came about because teachers in the school district couldn't afford to live there. Recruitment of good teachers is a difficult task made more so in areas like Santa Clara, where a teacher is unlikely to be able to afford decent rental housing, let alone buy a home. The connection of the housing affordability problem to Santa Clara's economy is so clear that private firms have funded the Santa Clara Housing Trust, also covered in this book. The long-term impact of the problem on recruitment and retention of employees is viewed as such a threat that private companies have donated millions of dollars to provide funding for housing for households of all income groups.

The Carrington development in Fairfax County, Virginia, provided workforce housing through the county's affordable dwelling unit ordinance. The ordinance came about because county leaders and residents realized that the people who are needed to make a community work were unable to live in the county they served. Many of the county's teachers, nurses, police officers, firefighters, and county employees needed to make a community function commuted in and out of the county every day.

In Camarilo, California, the California State University at Channel Islands was having difficulty recruiting staff and faculty due to the high cost of housing throughout California. Through the creative use of surplus land, they were able to construct market-rate apartments that supported an inventive program that allowed staff and faculty to buy homes in a new community developed on campus. While this provided a nice quality of life for staff and faculty, it also improved recruitment and retention efforts at the university.

Corporate leaders in Marshall, Minnesota, made the connection between housing and the economic health of their community. Schwan's Food, a major employer in the town, provided construction loans and funds for the construction of 128 units of affordable housing that will be occupied mainly be its employees. There is a growing realization nationally that while affordable housing has been viewed traditionally as an issue of social justice, it is also vital to the economic health of communities.

Strive for good planning and design to integrate affordable housing into existing communities.

Affordable housing is being developed with different principles than in previous decades. The very high-density development with interior corridors typical of the 1950s and 1960s has given way to lower-density designs with private entryways for each home to create a personal sense of ownership and security. While the overall density of affordable housing projects has gone down, it still must be built in a fairly dense fashion in order for the project to be financially feasible. Architects have been creative at disguising density through the strategic placement of open space, through the use of quadraplex configurations, and using topography and building construction to minimize the bulk of new construction.

Increasing community opposition and the emergence of mixed-income communities have created additional design dilemmas. New developments must fit into existing communities while often having a higher density than the surrounding areas due to the financial constraints created by restrictions on rent and sales prices. In mixed-income communities, efforts are made to integrate the affordable and market-rate units into a seamless community. All of these factors make the good design of affordable housing more important than ever for both the successful creation of livable and sustainable communities and to navigate the entitlement process.

The Edgemoore at Carrington development in Fairfax, Virginia, was required to provide eight units of workforce housing in a development of large-lot luxury homes, currently priced at over $1 million. Integrating eight townhouses selling for $120,000 each with million-dollar mansions was a design challenge to say the

least. The developer found an answer to the design dilemma in the "Great House" design. The eight units were constructed to look like two mansions, making them blend in with the existing community. The additional parking and services required for the units were moved to the rear of the site, further disguising the fact that the two buildings were actually eight dwelling units.

Several of the former public housing projects being redeveloped as mixed-income communities employ new urbanist design principles for several reasons. New urbanism is a proven way to deliver relatively high densities in a manner that is acceptable to most home-buyers and renters. The resulting sense of community created by the scale, detail, and proportions required by new urbanism also serves the goal of creating safe communities where neighbors can look out for one another.

The following case studies represent just 15 examples of how state and local government leaders and affordable housing developers have tried to address this difficult problem. There are countless other examples of best practices. Thankfully, there are people who continue to address this important issue day after day, constantly adjusting to the new political, financial, and social realities. The Fannie Mae Foundation and the Urban Land Institute hope this book encourages them to keep working on this problem, seeking ideas and innovations that can help solve America's affordable housing crisis.

Case Studies:

Successful Programs

S.M.A.R.T. Housing Initiative: Austin, Texas

Austin's S.M.A.R.T. Housing Initiative is an innovative self-funding program designed to increase the supply of affordable housing in Austin. An expedited and coordinated review process and a sliding scale of fee waivers are used to encourage development that is affordable, transit accessible, and green.

Year Enacted: 2000
Contact Information
Gina Copic, S.M.A.R.T. Housing Manager
City of Austin
Department of Neighborhood Housing and
Community Development
512-974-3180
regina.copic@ci.austin.tx.us
Census 2000 Figures
Population: 656,562
Median Income: $54,091
Median Home Value: $124,700
Homeownership Rate: 55 percent
Median Rent: $724

Summary: In 2000, the city of Austin created the Austin S.M.A.R.T. Housing Initiative to stimulate the production of housing for low- and moderate-income households in neighborhoods within the city limits. The residences built under the auspices of this program are intended to be safe, mixed income, accessible, reasonably priced, and transit oriented (thus the S.M.A.R.T. acronym) and meet Austin's "green" building standards. Eligible projects include single-lot and infill development as well as new subdivisions. Three incentives constitute the foundation of the S.M.A.R.T. Housing program: development fee waivers, expedited review by a designated team of S.M.A.R.T. Housing staff, and assistance from the S.M.A.R.T. Housing staff to resolve any development-related issues with other city departments.

Community Profile

Austin is the capital of Texas and the seat of Travis County. Located in the central Texas hill country, the city lies approximately 230 miles from Mexico and less than 200 miles from three of the ten largest U.S. cities (192 miles north to Dallas, 79 miles from San Antonio to the south, and 162 miles from Houston to the southeast).

Between 1980 and 2000, Austin's population nearly doubled, expanding from 345,496 in 1980 to 656,562 in 2000. During this time, the city's economic base grew from state and federal government and the University of Texas to include the high-technology field and research organizations. By 2010, Austin's population is projected to reach 800,000—representing a yearly increase of almost 19,000 people. While the city occupies a land area of 271.8 square miles, the greater Austin metropolitan area includes five counties and had a population of 1.3 million in 2002. In that year, the population was 52.9 percent white, 30.5 percent Hispanic, 9.8 percent African American, and 4.7 percent Asian, with other ethnic groups constituting the remaining 2.1 percent.

Affordable Housing Concerns

Austin's fast growth, especially during the 1990s, drove up housing prices rapidly and created problems with housing affordability. Between 1990 and 2000, the average price of a single-family home rose more than 120 percent, to $194,200. Rents increased by an average of 7 percent every year between 1990 and 1999, rising to $872 for a two-bedroom, two-bathroom unit by December 1999.[9]

According to the Community Action Network (CAN), an Austin-based advocacy group, only 53 percent of households could afford a median-priced home in metropolitan Austin in 2002. CAN also reports that half of all renters in the Austin metropolitan area could not afford the average two-bedroom apartment ($820 per month). In 2000, an Austin renter needed to earn at least $16 per hour to afford the average rent. In 1999, CAN published *Through the Roof,* a report documenting Austin's housing affordability problems that helped draw attention to the issue. By the mid-1990s, city leaders recognized the increasing problem of housing affordability in Austin and began to explore ways to address the issue.

History of Legislation

The establishment of the S.M.A.R.T. Housing Initiative followed several incremental steps to address growth patterns in the city. In 1997, the city expanded its development fee waiver program to include more fee waivers for both for-profit and nonprofit builders, applicable if all of the housing also met specified construction standards. The previous fee waiver program had long been available to nonprofit developers, and the fee waiver expansion was enacted to encourage the production of more affordable housing.

In 1998, the city of Austin adopted its smart growth initiative in an effort to manage future growth. In 2000, in an attempt to coordinate Austin's housing needs with its smart growth efforts, the city council adopted the S.M.A.R.T. Housing Initiative. The program, developed after a long exploration and public review process, sought to address the pattern of sprawl in the greater metropolitan area by making housing development within the city limits competitive with new suburban residential construction that typically faced lower land prices, less regulation, and shorter development time frames.

Key Program Components

S.M.A.R.T. Housing seeks to create reasonably priced housing in mixed-income communities that meet standards for safety, accessibility, transit-oriented development, and green building. Among the program goals are the following: to maximize the use of public resources to leverage private investment; to stimulate the development of housing on vacant lots in new and existing subdivisions; and to promote the use of the city's existing infrastructure and services.

The foundation of the S.M.A.R.T. Housing program consists of three incentives: fee waivers, expedited review, and advocacy to resolve development-related issues with other city departments.

To receive these benefits and incentives from the city, a project must meet S.M.A.R.T. Housing certification standards, including the following:

SAFE

Compliance with the city's land development and building codes.

MIXED INCOME/REASONABLY PRICED

A portion of the development must be "reasonably priced," i.e., affordable to households making up to 80 percent of AMI (about $56,900 for a family of four) and spending no more than 30 percent of their family income on housing.

ACCESSIBLE

Compliance with federal, state, and local accessibility standards, some of which are specific to the S.M.A.R.T. Housing program.

TRANSIT

Location of new development on either a major bus route or a proposed light-rail line.

GREEN

Conformance to a minimum level of Austin's green building standards.

Developers under the S.M.A.R.T. Housing Initiative are afforded three important incentives toward building affordable housing:

FEE WAIVERS

Developers of projects meeting S.M.A.R.T. Housing certification standards may receive waivers of the city's capital recovery fee, development review and inspection fee, and certain construction inspection fees. Developments of five or more residential units must include at least 10 percent reasonably priced housing to be eligible for full or partial waivers. All of the project's dwelling units must meet S.M.A.R.T. Housing standards for the waivers to apply. Fee waivers are linked to the percentage of reasonably priced units, as noted in the chart below.

A Builder Provides	The City of Austin Provides
10% S.M.A.R.T. reasonably priced units	25% fee waivers and fast-track review
20% S.M.A.R.T. reasonably priced units	50% fee waivers and fast-track review
30% S.M.A.R.T. reasonably priced units	75% fee waivers and fast-track review
40% S.M.A.R.T. reasonably priced units	100% fee waivers and fast-track review

Developments of four or fewer housing units are required to be 100 percent reasonably priced and meet all other S.M.A.R.T. Housing standards.

Fee waivers are currently limited to 1,000 housing units and are allocated on a first-come, first-served basis. Typical cost savings for housing produced under the S.M.A.R.T. Housing program are as follows: $600 per unit of multifamily housing and $2,000 per single-family house from fee waivers, as well as reduced carrying costs from the expedited review process.

EXPEDITED REVIEW

Developments that meet S.M.A.R.T. Housing standards are eligible for expedited review by a dedicated S.M.A.R.T. Housing review team, which typically is faster than the review time for conventional development projects. City staff works with applicants to move projects through review and inspection as quickly and efficiently as possible. In FY 2002–2003, the average completion time for S.M.A.R.T. Housing subdivision and site plan reviews was approximately half the time of conventional reviews.

ADVOCACY

S.M.A.R.T. Housing staff assists applicants in resolving development-related issues with other city departments. Staff is available to facilitate discussions and to find solutions.

Program Administration

Two city agencies are involved with the administration of the S.M.A.R.T. Housing program: the Austin Housing Finance Corporation (AHFC) and the Neighborhood Housing and Community Development (NHCD) Department.

The AHFC is the S.M.A.R.T. Housing Initiative's lead agency to foster partnerships with the homebuilding industry to produce and maintain affordable housing in the city of Austin, and provides the agency with the ability to acquire surplus city lands suitable for housing at below-market prices.

The Pedernales comprises 91 condominiums and 14 storefront commercial spaces for studios and offices. In addition to the mixed-use development, the project includes wide sidewalks and benches, a plaza, and a small park.

The Pedernales, developed with 40 percent "reasonably priced" units to meet S.M.A.R.T. Housing standards, provides live/work space for the local creative community that is close to downtown.

The Pedernales

Austin, Texas

Downtown Austin prides itself on its creative community—musicians, artists, filmmakers, entrepreneurs, and others. But gentrification and high housing costs have endangered this population in the central city.

Developers Richard DeVarga and Larry Warshaw have produced the $10 million Pedernales, a S.M.A.R.T. Housing development in east Austin, to provide live/work space for the local creative community close to downtown. Located on a three-acre site east of I-35 at the corner of Pedernales and East Sixth Street, the Pedernales offers housing aimed at accommodating the creative crowd with a combination of 91 condominiums (40 percent "reasonably priced," for S.M.A.R.T. Housing standards) and 14 storefront commercial spaces for studios and offices.

The development, sited on land formerly owned by Union Pacific Railroad, has housing prices ranging from about $100,000 for 680 square feet to just under $200,000 for 1,200 square feet—coming in at $150 a square foot, about half the cost of a similar downtown unit. The project sold out during the construction phase. In addition to the mixed-use development, the project includes wide sidewalks, benches, a plaza, and a small park.

The NHCD is the single point of contact to facilitate S.M.A.R.T. Housing developments, as well as the lead agency to foster partnerships with neighborhoods and to implement housing policy issues. The NHCD is responsible for coordinating with other municipal departments, which verify that S.M.A.R.T. Housing developments are consistent with applicable federal and city policies.

The S.M.A.R.T. Housing program is implemented by three staff members, plus a separate six-person review team to inspect eligible developments and keep the expedited review moving smoothly and quickly.

Program Effectiveness/Units Built

In the first year, program staff expected applications to build 600 housing units. Instead, applications representing the construction of 6,000 new housing units came in. In the three years before S.M.A.R.T. Housing was initiated, a total of roughly 325 new housing units that met city affordability and technical standards were completed. In the three years since the program was fully implemented (as of September 2004), more than 4,000 new housing units that met S.M.A.R.T. Housing standards have been completed.

Since its implementation, S.M.A.R.T. Housing reached a point where it dominates the multifamily construction market as well as an increasing portion of the single-family home market.

Year	Multifamily Units Completed	Single-Family Units Completed
2001	0	31
2002	1,108	274
2003	816	245
2004	1,013	599

An evaluation of the program has indicated that the fee waivers and expedited reviews are self-funding. Since projects are completed more quickly, completed housing units get into the tax base earlier than with slower, conventional review and associated revenue for the city-owned utilities is received earlier as well.

The program is drawing developers who had left to build in the suburbs back to the city—some builders have even requested annexation of a development into the city in order to be eligible to participate in S.M.A.R.T. Housing. The program is working for developers from a business point of view, as the fee waivers and faster review process are saving time on project completion and thus improving the project's return.

Challenges—Present and Future

Present and anticipated challenges for the S.M.A.R.T. Housing program include the following:

■ Evaluating whether the program will continue to be cost-effective for the city.

■ Encouraging the construction of S.M.A.R.T. Housing in underserved neighborhoods, especially those west of Interstate 35. In Austin, I-35 is a dividing boundary, and much of the housing that has been produced so far lies east of it, in the more affluent neighborhoods, with little new housing being produced west of the highway.

■ Continuing to address affordable housing needs if current conditions change significantly, e.g., an increase in construction costs or a rapid rise in interest rates.

■ Managing the decreasing amount of vacant land available within the city for new construction.

■ Maintaining affordability in rental and for-sale units over a longer time period.

The Housing Trust of Santa Clara County: Santa Clara County, California

The Housing Trust of Santa Clara County is distinguished from other housing trusts in that 43 percent of its funding comes from private sector firms, with companies like Applied Materials, Hewlett Packard, and Adobe Systems contributing over $1,000,000 each.

Year Enacted: 1998

Contact Information

Housing Trust of Santa Clara County
1786 Technology Drive
San Jose, California 95110
408-436-3454
info@housingtrustscc.org

Census 2000 Figures

Population: 1,678,421
Median Household Income: $74,335
Median Home Value: $446,400
Homeownership Rate: 59.8 percent
Median Monthly Rent: $1,185

Summary: The Housing Trust of Santa Clara County was established in 1998 in response to the housing shortage caused by the rapid expansion of the area's technology companies. With local housing prices among the highest in the country, the public and private sectors were recruited for donations to a housing trust. The trust has raised more than $30 million through March 2006, over 50 percent of which came from private sector sources. The trust administers three programs, each of which is intended to give immediate assistance to different target groups. The First-Time Homebuyer Program offers zero-interest loans to help cover closing costs, and has assisted 1,450 families in purchasing their first home. The Multifamily Rental Program provides short- and long-term loans at low interest rates to nonprofit developers of affordable rental housing. The Multifamily Rental Program has made 17 loans to 16 developments, resulting in 1,275 new affordable units. The Homeless and Special Needs Program is similar to the Multifamily Rental Program, but makes loans for developments targeted toward specific groups in need. The Homeless and Special Needs Program has made 18 loans that have sheltered 745 people in housing ranging from homeless shelters to inexpensive apartments for those living with HIV/AIDS. In total, the trust has invested $21.5 million, directly helping to create 3,470 affordable units whose total value exceeds $955 million.

Community Profile

Santa Clara County is located in the southern portion of the San Francisco Bay Area of California. With a population of nearly 1.7 million, it is the sixth most populous county in California, and the 14th most populous in the United States. The largest city is San Jose, with about 850,000 people. Santa Clara County lies at the center of Silicon Valley, which has the largest concentration of technology, information, and Internet companies in the country. Silicon Valley's employment base grew at a quick but steady pace from 1975 to 1995 as demand for technology products and services grew. During the mid-1990s, companies focusing on Internet services and e-commerce sprang up. Funded by large amounts of venture capital, these companies enjoyed a "boom" period that lasted until 2001. This technology and Internet boom brought hundreds of thousands of jobs to Silicon Valley and Santa Clara County. In 2001, a lack of investor confidence and a failure to generate meaningful profits pushed many Internet companies to the brink of bankruptcy.

The prevalence of the high-tech industry has had profound impacts on the county's housing and economy. Job creation far outpaced housing construction, leading to a housing shortage. Over 125,000 workers (one-sixth of the workforce) commuted from neighboring Alameda and San Mateo counties. Traffic congestion, the prevailing road network, and Santa Clara County's sheer size of 1,291 square miles all lead to long and difficult commutes for most residents. A portion of the county's workforce is extraordinarily well educated and well compensated by the standards of most other communities. Forty-two percent of county residents have a bachelor's degree and 17 percent hold a postgraduate degree. The area median income is $74,335. Young people with the right skills can command high salaries for in-demand jobs in software engineering and Internet technology. Householders aged 25 to 34 earn a median income of $77,250, only $5,000 less than those aged 45 to 54. However, the housing shortage and resulting exorbitant home prices makes the possibility of owning a home close to work unreachable to many of these highly paid professionals. In most any other American city, a person earning $77,000 a year could choose to purchase almost any home of their choice.

Most industries—and all communities—require workers of all skill levels and incomes. Even the wealthiest city requires workers to cook food, staff cash registers, clean floors, and do yardwork. The housing situation for workers on the lower end of the wage scale can only be described as dire. For them, just finding adequate affordable rental housing requires living outside of Santa Clara County.

Affordable Housing Concerns

High housing costs had been a concern of local civic leaders and housing advocates for many years. Local employers joined the call for reform at the end of the decade, perceiving that high housing costs were stifling their ability to recruit and retain top-notch employees. The technology job growth in Santa Clara County, already an exclusive and expensive area, further compounded affordability problems. While these new jobs brought higher salaries, they also resulted in brutal increases in housing costs. From 1995 to 2000, only one new housing unit was being created for every 4.2 new jobs. The resulting shortage of housing led to an uptick in home prices and rental rates. Price increases reached as high as 34.5 percent between March 1999 and March 2000. The county estimates that fewer than 2,000 units of affordable housing were built between 1980 and 2000, and there were few programs or agencies with the capability to build more.

Murphy Ranch
Morgan Hill, Santa Clara County, California

Murphy Ranch was developed using funds from the Homeless and Special Needs Program. Located in Morgan Hill, a community of million-dollar large-lot homes, the 100-unit complex features two-, three-, and four-bedroom townhomes on 7.2 acres. First Community Housing, a San Jose–based affordable housing developer, cobbled together financing from nine different sources to fund the project. The Housing Trust of Santa Clara County awarded the project a $500,000 long-term loan at 2 percent interest. Construction began in June 2003 and was completed in October 2004.

The various funding sources required different income restrictions. Rents are scaled to be affordable to households earning between 22 and 60 percent of the area median income. Monthly rents range from $383 to $1,126 for a two-bedroom townhouse. To ease the burden on bigger families, larger townhomes are only moderately more expensive—renting from $492 to $1,449 a month.

First Community Housing specializes in eco-friendly, or "green," affordable housing. All units at Murphy Ranch are built to exceed California's Title 24 green building standards. Energy is saved through the use of solar panels, insulating windows, and combination water and air heaters. Recycled materials and non-toxic finishes add to the eco-friendliness of the development and helped qualify the project for certain tax credits. In cooperation with the local transit agency, passes are distributed that allow for free transit rides on all county bus and light rail lines. Besides their direct impact on the environment, these measures help reduce the cost of housing for tenants through lower utility bills and transportation costs.

Many experts predicted a housing price drop-off after the end of the technology bubble. Those predictions have not materialized. Many jobs created during the technology run-up have remained, although many companies have ceased hiring new employees. While median home price increases have slowed, they continue to appreciate at double-digit rates. The median single-family home in Santa Clara County now costs over $600,000, one of the most expensive in the country. On the other hand, rental prices have declined since the technology downturn. A typical one-bedroom apartment now rents for around $900 monthly, with vacancy rates in the low double digits, off from a high of over $1,400 a month. Whether this rental decline is due to employment changes or the success of the Housing Trust in stimulating multifamily construction is difficult to determine.

With home prices continually spiraling upward, some important groups were priced out of the housing market. Many educated technology employees commanded the monthly salary necessary to afford the average home, but lacked the $40,000 to $60,000 savings required for a downpayment. Civic employees such as teachers, postal workers, and firefighters were being paid more than their nationwide peers, but their salaries were not enough to keep pace with the housing market. Attracting and retaining talented civil servants was a serious issue for local governments. Service workers such as retail clerks, janitors, and wait staff found it difficult or impossible to both live and work in Santa Clara County.

Governments and private sector firms in Santa Clara County faced a crisis of labor. Without affordable housing, it was possibile that talented and qualified workers would becoming unwilling to move to Silicon Valley. Even more pressing was the shortage of service-sector workers. These low-wage workers were demanding ever-increasing salaries to keep pace with ever-increasing housing costs. Many types of businesses depend on low wages to maintain profits. Without a program to soften the housing situation, Santa Clara County risked stagnating job growth or, even worse, an exodus of employers.

The 100 townhomes of Murphy Ranch provide an affordable rental option in one of the most expensive housing markets in the country.

History of Program

Representatives of the private sector, the public sector, and nonprofit organizations came together to form the Housing Trust of Santa Clara County in 1998 to quickly advance the development of affordable housing. The idea of a housing trust emerged over the course of a research study into housing by the Silicon Valley Manufacturing Group (SVMG). SVMG joined with community action groups such as the Housing Action Coalition and the Housing Leadership Council to lobby the county government and local foundations for funding to support affordable housing construction.

Most housing trusts are funded primarily through government sources. The Housing Trust of Santa Clara County is unique in that it is primarily funded by private sector donations.

The trust set a goal of raising a $20 million endowment to provide ongoing support of affordable housing programs. Contributions were received from employers, nonprofit foundations, private citizens, the county government, and all 15 municipalities in the county. The goal of $20 million was reached within two years. Since 2001, donations have slowed, in large part due to the sluggish economy of the region. Since its inception, just over $30 million has been donated to the trust.

Donations from the private sector accounted for about 50 percent of the trust's income. Well-known technology companies like Applied Materials, Hewlett Packard, and Adobe Systems contributed over $1,000,000 each. Computer chip maker Intel gave the first million-dollar donation in the fall of 2000. Through matching donations, some employers encouraged their employees to give to the trust. Local citizens contribute outside of corporate donation programs through small donations of $20 and up. Recipients of homebuyer assistance frequently donate cash to the program, in appreciation of the trust rescuing them from the peculiar position of having disposable income but being unable to purchase a home without assistance. Since it is a 501(c) nonprofit organization, donations to the trust are tax deductible.

Approximately 30 percent of the trust's money was appropriated from local governments. Santa Clara County started the campaign with a $2 million donation. Eventually, all 15 of the county's municipalities contributed to the trust. There is no dedicated funding source for the trust, and donations do not renew annually. In some cases, appropriations from municipalities were one-time-only gifts. In November 2003, California voters passed Proposition 46, a measure that approved bond sales to match fundraising by housing trusts. Santa Clara raised $2.4 million, which was matched with $2

Murphy Ranch was constructed as a "green" affordable housing community, exceeding California green building standards. The community pool shown here is solar heated.

million from Proposition 46 funds, the maximum allowed. Local nonprofit groups donated the remaining 10 percent of the trust's resources.

Key Program Components

The Housing Trust Fund of Santa Clara County runs three housing programs: 1) the First-Time Homebuyer Assistance Program; 2) the Multifamily Rental Housing Program; and 3) the Homeless and Special Needs Housing Program. All three programs are funded from a pool of money held by the Housing Trust of Santa Clara County, a 501(c) not-for-profit, charitable organization. The trust does not have a dedicated, permanent funding source. It depends on voluntary contributions from local governments, corporations, private citizens, and local foundations.

The First-Time Homebuyer Assistance Program offers loans to help cover the closing costs associated with purchasing a home, a major roadblock for many families. These zero-interest loans are for up to $6,500 each, and must be repaid to the trust upon sale of the home, or refinancing of the original mortgage. To qualify for a first-time homebuyer loan, the purchaser must not have owned a home in Santa Clara County during the previous year. The buyer must secure a mortgage from a participating lender that allows downpayment assistance from the trust. Finally, the buyer's gross household income must not exceed 120 percent of the area median income for Santa Clare County. In addition, the home price cannot exceed $550,000.

The Housing Trust's Multifamily Program was established to make loans to developers of affordable rental units. The Housing Trust has designated these funds to provide four types of financing: land or property acquisition loans, predevelopment loans, bridge loans, and debt service coverage guarantees. Provided that they meet minimum eligibility requirements, acquisition loans, construction gap loans, and debt service guarantees are available on a rolling first-come, first-served basis. Priority is given only to projects in geographic areas that are underserved by affordable rental housing. Long-term construction or gap loans are awarded on a rolling, competitive basis. The maximum loan amount is $500,000, and is usually

awarded on a per-affordable-unit basis. Loans carry a 2 percent interest rate, an additional 2 percent origination fee, and range in term from 24 months for short-term loans to 30 years for long-term loans.

All multifamily loans are subject to a series of eligibility requirements. All developments must be sponsored by a nonprofit or governmental organization. Further, all developers must have demonstrated experience with building affordable housing. Developers must have local public and governmental support for the project. Each loan recipient must reserve at least 25 percent of the total units in the complex for families earning 50 percent or less of the area median income. The developer must enter into a "use agreement" that guarantees the affordable nature of the units for a specified length of time. Finally, the development must comply with four smart growth criteria as defined by the Silicon Valley Housing Action Coalition: 1) average density of 14 units per acre; 2) located within a municipality's urban service area; 3) located no more than a half mile from a commercial center and transit service; and 4) designed to complement existing neighborhoods with pedestrian-friendly design and the capacity for mixed use.

The Homeless and Special Needs Program is similar to the Multifamily Rental Program, except it targets housing for underserved and needy populations. The same developer requirements apply, except units must be reserved for households earning 35 percent of the area median income. Projects can be approved under the Homeless and Special Needs Program if they target at-risk groups such as victims of domestic violence, seniors, individuals with HIV/AIDS, homeless persons, and the physically or mentally disabled.

Program Administration

The trust endeavors to expend all of its assets into the community. However, the zero-interest first-time homebuyer loans and the 2 percent multifamily loans are not a sustainable source of income for the trust. It could take up to 30 years for the principal amount to be repaid. In the case of first-time homebuyer loans, the amount paid will be the same amount lent, but the money will be less valuable due to inflation. The repayment of these loans will give the trust some sustainability in future decades, but it does not create much on-hand cash in the short term. This is why the trust must continuously raise funds.

The trust attempts to minimize its overhead and administration expenses by maintaining a small staff. There are five full-time employees: an executive director, a development/fundraising manager, a comptroller, an accountant, and a program assistant. Two part-time employees help fill the gap: a communications/public relations director and a receptionist. The trust's Web site informs users of the requirements to file applications for closing cost loans and multifamily rental loans. Application materials and a link to donate money are also found on the trust's Web site.

Program Effectiveness/Units Built

The three programs administered by the Housing Trust of Santa Clara County have created a total of 5,310 housing opportunities for county residents. The First-Time Homebuyer Program has helped 1,450 families pay for closing costs on their homes. The average price of homes purchased under the program was $348,699, and household income averaged $69,892. The majority of homes purchased with closing cost assistance have been condominium units. The trust has been able to fund every qualified application for assistance.

The Multifamily Rental Housing Program has lent $6.1 million to developers of rental housing. The 17 loans made under this program have leveraged $341 million in total development from other sources, and have resulted in the creation of 1,275 housing units. The Homeless and Special Needs Housing Program has created 745 units of housing by making 18 loans to developers worth $5.1 million. Homeless prevention grants worth $382,513 have helped provide temporary shelter for 1,840 people.

The trust has made it possible for a sizable number of people to purchase homes. Promoting homeownership not only assists the recipient families, but also helps the overall community. Since new homeowners are more likely to stay in the community over the long term, the program also helps foster a stable workforce. And the multifamily rental program helps local businesses attract and retain talented workers who otherwise could not afford to live in Santa Clara County.

Challenges—Present and Future

The greatest challenge for the Housing Trust of Santa Clara County will be to sustain its funding levels through donations or secure other sources of permanent funding. Corporate donations have trailed off considerably since 2001, as technology companies increasing find themselves strapped for cash. The future of large donations likely lies with increased funding from local jurisdictions and the state of California. The trust is currently seeking a dedicated funding source to ensure that programs can continue in perpetuity.

Santa Clara County is quickly running out of available land. About one-third of the county is in conservation holdings or is otherwise undevelopable. The remaining two-thirds is already urbanized. Infill development is playing an increasingly important role in providing housing opportunities.

Eventually, the technology sector will recover from its recent fall. The housing climate has the potential to impede the ability of new companies to establish themselves in Santa Clara County. By reining in its high housing costs, the county can ensure that it remains the center of the new, technology-driven economy. If housing costs remain out of control, the county risks losing jobs to other areas.

Moderately Priced Dwelling Unit (MPDU) Program: Montgomery County, Maryland

One of the first and most successful inclusionary zoning programs in the country, Montgomery County's MPDU program requires most new development to include an affordable component. The program has led to a dispersal of affordable housing units throughout the county and provided low- to moderate-income families access to high-quality communities and services.

Year Enacted: 1976

Contact Information
Montgomery County Department of Housing and Community Affairs
Moderately Priced Housing Program
100 Maryland Avenue, Fourth Floor
Rockville, Maryland 20850
240-777-3705
http://www.montgomerycountymd.gov/DHCA

Housing Opportunities Commission of Montgomery County
10400 Detrick Avenue
Kensington, Maryland 20895
301-929-6700
http://www.hocmc.org

Census 2000 Figures
Population: 873,341
Household Income: $71,551
Median Home Value: $221,800
Median Monthly Rent: $914

Summary: The MPDU program is a mandatory inclusionary zoning program that requires developers to reserve up to 15 percent of all built units for affordable housing use. Montgomery County imposes price restrictions for ten years on owned homes and up to 20 years on rental units. The MPDU program markets units to renters and first-time homebuyers with incomes ranging from under $16,000 up to $49,000 for families of four or more people. Prices of homes range from $85,000 to $135,000, and are adjusted annually to ac-

count for inflation, cost of living, and construction costs. Over 11,500 dwelling units have been produced under the program, making it the most productive inclusionary zoning program in the nation.

Community Profile

Montgomery County, Maryland, lies directly northwest of the District of Columbia, bordered on its western edge by the Potomac River. Once an agricultural area, the county began suburbanizing in the 1890s with the arrival of trolley-car lines from downtown Washington. After World War II, the greater Washington area experienced rapid population growth, which spread quickly into the counties bordering the District of Columbia. For decades, Montgomery County has served as a high-income suburb of Washington, D.C. In more recent years, the county has shed its "bedroom community" image, as economic development efforts have brought in more employers. Today, almost 60 percent of residents work within the county.

During the last two decades, the county's population has been diversifying. Minority populations accounted for only 8 percent of the population in 1970. By 2000, 40 percent of the county's 873,000 residents were non-white. The housing stock has also diversified, and today townhouses and multifamily units make up almost half of all dwelling units.

Over the last 60-plus years, Montgomery County has earned a sound reputation for comprehensive, imaginative, and aggressive planning and growth management. The county has designated the northern third of its land as a farmland protection area, and promotes its conservation through transferable development rights. The development corridors are centered on I-270 and U.S. 29. Those corridors are served by 18.5 miles of the Washington Metrorail system. Over the past five years, there has been substantial transit-oriented development around the 11 Metro stations in Montgomery County.

Affordable Housing Concerns

Like many other jurisdictions viewed as desirable places to live, Montgomery County has experienced a continuing increase in housing prices over several decades. In 2004, the median sales price for a single-family house or townhouse was $365,000.[10] Prices for older homes in some areas near the District of Columbia were escalating by 10 to 20 percent a year. Overall, Montgomery County is considered an affluent suburb, as the annual household income there was nearly $71,500 in 2000.[11]

The MPDU program was never intended to be—nor has it ever been—a social welfare program. The target recipients of MPDUs are moderate-income professionals such as police officers, teachers, and municipal employees. Attracting and retaining talented people is essential for providing high-quality services to county residents. Starting salaries for teachers and police officers are about 70 percent of the county median income—far too low to afford a median-priced home.[12] Without adequate housing, civic professionals are forced to spend a large percentage of their income on housing, or live elsewhere and face a long commute. Either of these conditions leads to high rates of turnover and low productivity among the most essential of workers.[13, 14] The county responded by instituting the MPDU program to provide both owned and rental housing to these essential members of the community.

History of Legislation

As early as the 1960s, citizen groups were concerned about the diminishing supply of affordable housing, especially for lower-income workers migrating to Montgomery County. In 1970, a grass-roots coalition led by the League of Women Voters and Suburban Maryland Fair Housing encouraged the county council to require builders to supply a share of all units in new residential developments at affordable prices—an inclusionary zoning program.

The MPDU legislation was introduced in the spring of 1972, and the county council worked for over a year to amend the legislation and assuage concerns over the bill. A key component was writing the law to emphasize providing affordable housing for young working families rather than overcoming racial and economic exclusion. Developers were given compensatory "density bonuses"

to deflect lawsuits that had arisen when nearby Fairfax County, Virginia, enacted an inclusionary zoning law. The council unanimously approved the bill in October 1973. A veto from the county executive was overridden, and the measure became law in January 1974. The first MPDUs were completed in 1976. Since then, the MPDU law has been modified more than 20 times. Almost every facet of the law has been changed at least once to address the changing situation of housing stock, developers, available land, and the general economy.

Key Program Components

At the heart of the MPDU program is the requirement that any development comprising over 35 units located in areas zoned for half-acre or smaller lots must set aside a certain percentage of built units as affordable. For many years the threshold was 50 units, but reductions in parcel sizes and the scale of developments necessitated a change. Currently, developers must set aside 15 percent of built units for the MPDU program, up from 12.5 percent a few years ago. Affordable units must be mixed in with market-rate units, and their exteriors cannot appear different. Interiors are allowed to have minor variations, such as inexpensive fixtures and flooring. In general, MPDU status is tied to an individual dwelling unit. Price controls cannot be "floated" between units within a development. Forty percent of the for-sale MPDUs must be made available for sale to the Housing Opportunities Commission (HOC), which administers the county's public housing subsidy programs.

Developers who set aside units for the MPDU program receive up to a 22 percent density bonus above the density allowed in the zoning ordinance. In areas zoned for single-family detached homes, up to 60 percent of the affordable units can be in attached homes. Density bonuses allow developers to build more units in denser settings, which in turn enables them to recoup expenses incurred when constructing MPDUs. Allowing greater densities makes it possible for developers to mix single-family homes with multifamily residences. MPDU density bonuses are also a de facto transit-oriented development (TOD) program, as development hotspots around Metrorail stations can be designed in a more concentrated configuration.

An owner who resells an MPDU home does not retain the entire amount of appreciation (MPDUs cannot be leased or subleased). If an MPDU unit is resold during the price control period, the owner receives his or her equity in the home plus fair market value for improvements and inflation. The home is then resold to a new owner at current MPDU prices. At the end of the price control period, the home can be sold at market value. The profit between purchase price and sale price is split between the owner and the county. In the case where an owner keeps the home for the entire price control period, the appreciation is split 50-50. For owners who keep the home for less than ten years, a prorated amount of the appreciation goes to the owner.

MPDUs are held under price control. Rental units remain under price controls for ten to 20 years. Rents are adjusted each year to be affordable for people living at 65 percent of the area median income or less. Rent is paid to the owner of the property, and the county does not make up the difference between MPDU and market rents. Renters may stay indefinitely, but if their income

rises above the cutoff they must find new housing. At the end of the rental price control period, landlords may rent units at market rate.

For-sale homes are also held under price controls for ten years. Households making less than 75 percent of the county median income are allowed to purchase MPDU homes, and the sale price is adjusted annually by the county. Currently, detached homes are being sold for $54 per square foot, or about $135,000 for the average 2,500-square-foot home. The allowed price per square foot rises as homes are built more densely, and high-rise condominiums can be sold for $119 per square foot. MPDU sales prices were raised about 10 percent in 2004 to help developers recoup rising expenses, particularly costs related to construction.

Applicants for home purchase must attend a homebuyer education course and undergo credit and criminal background checks. To guarantee impartiality, a third-party, nonprofit group performs background checks and administers education courses. Homebuyers can secure private financing or may qualify for below-market-rate

The 70 townhouses at Potomac Glen are moderately priced dwelling units (MPDUs) that were required as part of the 560-unit development, located three miles west of Rockville and constructed in 1996. Price restrictions will be removed from the homes in 2006.

loans from the Housing Opportunities Commission. Once eligibility to apply has been established, applicants are ranked in a point system with preference given to MPDU renters and longtime county residents.

Some developers choose to negotiate an alternative agreement in which a cash payment or land dedication is given to the county in lieu of placing units under price control. Cash payments are directed to the Housing Opportunities Commission, which uses the funds to make below-market-rate loans and provide public housing. Developers have used these "alternative agreements" when constructing very expensive units to opt out of the MPDU program. Developers choosing to make cash payments are not awarded a density bonus over the parcel's zoned density. Allowing developers to negotiate alternative agreements has been a topic of political and public contention in recent years. Some sectors of the public contend that alternative agreements violate the spirit of the MPDU law.

Program Administration

The MPDU program is administered through the county's Department of Housing and Community Affairs. The county's office is responsible for setting MPDU prices, maintaining listings of new and resale units, choosing new program participants, and ensuring the construction of new MPDUs. Three people, including two professional planners, staff the MPDU office. The county spends $270,000 annually to administer the program.

The HOC administers most of Montgomery County's housing programs. It was founded in 1966 to administer federal funds to support substandard housing rehabilitation and low-income housing. The 1972 Moderately Priced Dwelling Unit law created several mechanisms to support the mission of the HOC. The MPDU law guarantees that up to 40 percent of new affordable units may be sold to the HOC. The HOC also provides

below-market-rate loans to homebuyers. The HOC has amassed a widely dispersed and varied portfolio of public housing to rent to low- and very low-income families in Montgomery County. Today, the HOC administers 15 separate housing programs with a budget of over $183 million. The HOC owns, manages, and administers 12,431 units, of which about 6,000 are dedicated to the Housing Choice Voucher Program (Section 8). Without the dedicated revenue stream and the guaranteed option to purchase affordable units, the HOC would not be able to provide so many affordable units to Montgomery County's lowest-income residents.

Program Effectiveness/Units Built

As of early 2004, over 11,500 MPDUs have been produced. About 8,100 units were produced for sale, of which just under 2,000 remain under price controls.

Fifteen of the townhomes at Potomac Glen were sold to Montgomery County's Housing Opportunities Commission to be occupied by low-income households. The remaining townhomes were sold to qualifying moderate-income households at sales prices ranging from $89,000 to $95,000.

Three thousand four hundred rental MPDUs have been built, and 850 remain price restricted. Many former MPDUs have been released into the general housing stock at the end of their price-control period. The remainder were purchased by the HOC to build the county's public housing stock. The MPDU program has been a success at placing the beneficiaries of the program in high-quality housing at a reasonable price. However, the MPDU program appears to have had little or no effect on housing prices countywide.

The county has attempted to further improve the effectiveness of the program by modifying some of its attributes. The threshold of development size has been reduced from 50 to 35, and the county is considering reducing it further. As mentioned before, the percentage of units that must be dedicated was increased to 15 percent. Officials have also considered extending the price control periods.

Challenges—Present and Future

The housing situation in Montgomery County is often a topic in local elections. Few local politicians take positions against the MPDU program. Most are concerned with making changes to the program to help create more MPDUs or help developers. Recent discussions have included devoting surplus county property on which to build MPDU units. Surplus properties are scattered throughout the county, and many are in excellent housing locations. There is little doubt that the MPDU program will continue far into the future, as it enjoys strong political and popular support. One area of strong support for the MPDU program is its ability to support substantial publicly subsidized housing programs for little or no public dollars.

As housing prices continue to rise, the income division between neighbors becomes more pronounced. This is manifesting itself in several ways. For example, luxury condominiums require a large owner fee for upkeep and operations. This fee is not subject to affordability controls, and can put condominium ownership out of reach for many in need. Further, developers of high-end housing are increasingly choosing to make alternative agreements—such as cash payments—instead of building MPDUs.

The greatest challenge of the MPDU program will be to sustain its success. The sustainability of the program depends on continued growth, since new MPDUs are created only when a housing development is constructed. As price controls end after ten or 20 years, affordable units are taken away. When development slows, fewer and fewer affordable units will be available. About 75 percent of the developable land in Montgomery County has been built out. Of Montgomery County's 19 municipalities, only the city of Rockville participates in the MPDU program. Prime developable lands near major activity centers such as Metrorail are largely built on. The future success of the MPDU program depends on the county's ability to foster infill growth, especially transit-oriented development.

Chapter 40B—the Comprehensive Permit Law: Commonwealth of Massachusetts

Also known as the "Anti-Snob Zoning Law."

The commonwealth of Massachusetts has set as a goal having 10 percent of the housing stock in every town in the commonwealth affordable to households making 80 percent or less of the area median income. In towns that do not meet this requirement, Chapter 40B—the Comprehensive Permit Law—allows developers to circumvent the zoning ordinance of local governments when a certain percentage of the proposed units in their development are designated as affordable.

> **Year Enacted:** 1969
> **Contact Information**
> Department of Housing and Community Development
> 1 Congress Street
> Tenth Floor
> Boston, Massachusetts 02114
> 617-727-7765
> http://www.state.ma.us/dhcd
> **Census 2000 Figures**
> Population: 6,349,097
> Median Household Income: $50,502
> Median Home Value: $185,700
> Homeownership Rate: 61.7 percent
> Median Monthly Rent: $684

Summary: Chapter 40B of the Massachusetts Administrative Code—also known as the "Anti-Snob Zoning Law"—allows developers of affordable housing to go through an alternative, streamlined approval process that removes zoning roadblocks to affordable housing construction. If 20 to 25 percent of the proposed units will have long-term affordability restrictions and the developer agrees to no more than 20 percent profit, the development qualifies under Chapter 40B. Local zoning

boards of appeal (ZBAs) are empowered to give all required approvals to such developments. ZBAs are authorized to implement less stringent requirements than set forth in the town's zoning ordinance. If a developer and ZBA cannot reach a compromise agreement or the application is rejected, the decision can be appealed to the state Housing Appeals Committee (HAC). Towns where 10 percent of the housing stock is affordable are exempt from the process.

Since its enactment in 1969, more than 30,000 units have been constructed in over 200 communities as a result of this law. Since some of these developments are mixed-income communities, it is estimated that 22,000 of the 30,000 total units have been reserved for households making 80 percent of the AMI or less.

Community Profile

With 6.3 million residents, Massachusetts is the nation's 13th most populous state, despite being the 44th largest in size. Core urban areas of the commonwealth are quite old. The capital, Boston, is also the largest city, and its suburbs extend beyond the state line into neighboring New Hampshire and Rhode Island. Massachusetts is home to several renowned institutions of higher learning, and as a result has a highly educated workforce of doctors, scientists, and researchers.

Urban sprawl and large-lot residential homes pose a dual threat to the commonwealth of Massachusetts's housing affordability. Massachusetts is already a geographically small state, and many cities and towns compound the issue of land availability by imposing zoning ordinances with large lot requirements, among other exclusionary zoning policies. Many towns in the eastern half of the state are widely known for their exclusivity. Developable land is at a premium, so future population growth and affordable housing construction is dependent on promoting infill and redevelopment.

Affordable Housing Concerns

Massachusetts has some of the most expensive housing in the United States. In eastern parts of the commonwealth, median home prices exceed $350,000, and virtually no market-rate homes can be purchased for under $250,000. While prices in western Massachusetts are somewhat more reasonable, housing markets in attractive areas such as along highways or near employment centers remain very high. Rents have been increasing at a steady pace as well. Greater Boston has experienced a 40 percent rise in apartment rental rates since 1998, with prices reaching over $1,200 a month for a modest two-bedroom apartment. Housing prices have become burdensome for middle-income families, let alone for those with lower income.

A task force established in February 2003 (see feature box) to conduct a comprehensive review of Chapter 40B stated that "the lack of affordable housing in Massachusetts continues to be the greatest threat to our economic vitality." The task force goes on to say that if the affordable housing crisis in the Commonwealth continues unabated, "Massachusetts will continue to lose population and fail to attract and retain highly skilled labor."[15] The governor himself has declared that "the number-one complaint I heard from corporate CEOs is that the cost of housing is too high in Massachusetts." He reiterated that "unless we are able to produce more housing that is affordable to people across a broad range of incomes, the state will be at a long-term economic disadvantage."[16]

Many local zoning codes mandate minimum lot sizes for single-family homes or ban multifamily residential development altogether. Other codes may enforce external building features, footprint requirements, and parking provision. Local governments nationwide have long used tactics such as these to exclude members of lower-income groups from their communities in the name of "preserving neighborhood character." Chapter 40B is commonly referred to as the "Anti-Snob Zoning Law," reflecting its ability to circumvent zoning practices whose legislative intent is to exclude certain people, not protect the community or its citizenry. Developers simply are not financially able to construct affordable housing—or even inexpensive market-rate housing—under zoning regulations that require large homes on big lots.

History of Legislation

Chapter 40B was enacted in 1969 to address local regulatory barriers to the construction of low- and moderate-income housing. The commonwealth set a goal of making 10 percent of its housing stock affordable to households making 80 percent or less than the area median income. Towns may use any number of programs to reach the 10 percent affordable goal.

Relatively little about the law has changed over the past 37 years. The core issues of the alternate review and appeals process remain generally the same. Some modifications have been made to what kinds of developers and projects qualify under Chapter 40B for expedited approval. Recent legislative action has been directed toward giving more rights to towns if they adopt an affordable housing plan and make significant progress toward the commonwealth's goal of 10 percent affordable housing stock. Other legislative actions allow for a more diverse set of housing types such as dormitory rooms, mobile homes, and charitable housing to count toward the 10 percent requirement.

Towns have responded by implementing programs to build more affordable housing. For example, a number of towns have subsidized or promoted "friendly" Chapter 40B. In a friendly Chapter 40B, towns and developers agree on all aspects of the project but do not seek a permanent change to the future land use map.

Key Program Components

To qualify for approval under Chapter 40B, a development must be approved or funded by an affordable housing program administered by a state agency, federal agency, or private housing trust fund. The development must have long-term (i.e., more than 15 years) affordability controls on at least 25 percent of planned units. These units must be priced to be affordable to households earning 80 percent of the AMI. Alternatively, developers may implement affordability controls on 20 percent of planned units if they will serve households earning 50 percent of the AMI. Developers must be a nonprofit organization; a governmental or quasi-governmental agency; or a "limited partnership" that agrees to less than a 20 percent profit margin. Any unexpected profit over 20 percent is paid directly to the town. Nonprofit and limited-partnership developers welcome the reduction in the time and expense of development approval.

Chapter 40B allows affordable housing developers to circumvent the zoning ordinances of local governments. To do so, local zoning boards of appeal (ZBAs) are authorized to grant all locally required approvals for development. ZBAs are also authorized by Chapter 40B to implement more flexible standards in lieu of the standing zoning ordinance. The result is a more streamlined and less costly approval process that lifts cost-prohibitive zoning requirements. A development submitted under Chapter 40B is rejected or approved by the ZBA. In this way, the ZBA approval process attempts to create consensus between developers of affordable housing and the town. The ZBA may impose design, density, or other requirements on the development, so long as those conditions do not make the development economically infeasible. The ZBA can also require that up to 70 percent of affordable units be reserved for local residents. If the developer and the ZBA cannot come to an agreement, the application can be rejected. However, if the ZBA rejects the application, the decision can be appealed to the state Housing Appeals Committee (HAC).

Developers have 20 days to appeal a rejected application to the HAC. The first hearing of an appeal is held in conjunction with a site visit, with subsequent hearings held in Boston. The full HAC meets four times each year to rule on appealed cases. The committee holds the same powers as local ZBAs, and can accept, accept with conditions, or reject an application for development submitted under Chapter 40B.

An average of 13 applications are appealed to the HAC each year. The HAC encourages parties to negotiate outside of hearings, and a significant number of cases are mediated before the hearing date. Since 1970, 24 percent of cases were successfully mediated between the town and the developer after appeal but before HAC ruling. Forty-five percent of appealed cases are withdrawn or dismissed. Only 31 percent (four per year) of appealed cases are decided by the HAC. Of those cases decided by hearings, the committee sided with the developer 84 percent of the time. The HAC regularly rejects proposed developments in towns that legitimately provide for affordable housing through local programs and comprehensive plans.

Proposed affordable housing developments are not without regulation. The ZBA takes into account comments from other city boards. Any comprehensive permit issued by the ZBA sets forth the conditions with which the developer must comply. Permits mandated under state law such as building safety, septic systems, and wetlands protection are still required of Chapter 40B projects.

Constructing affordable housing under Chapter 40B can place developers and towns in adversarial positions. The law rewards towns that are proactive in building and encouraging affordable housing production by exempting them from the process. Developers cannot use Chapter 40B if the town's housing stock is 10 percent affordable, or if affordable housing's land area occupies 1.5 percent of the town. However, the supply of affordable housing is not static. Affordable units come off price control after varying periods of time, and other units are lost to natural calamity and demolition. Towns must constantly monitor and adjust their housing supply accordingly if they seek to avoid the Chapter 40B process.

Program Administration

Very little state money or effort need be expended to implement Chapter 40B. Local governments handle the vast majority of development proposals with their in-house planning and zoning staffs. The only dedicated positions at the state level related to Chapter 40B are on the Housing Appeals Committee, since local governments handle the negotiation and approval of most Chapter 40B developments. State employees at the Department of Housing and Community Affairs provide an informational clearinghouse as well as best-practice examples for developers and towns to follow if they choose.

The HAC consists of a five-member board appointed jointly by the governor and the director of the State Department of Housing and Community Development. The chair of the committee is a full-time employee who chairs all hearings and writes all committee decisions. The other four board members convene approximately four times each year to deliberate and render decisions on appeals. One full-time legal counsel and a clerk also staff the HAC.

Local governments carry most of the administrative and financial burden of the Chapter 40B statute. Local staff must process applications and hold their ZBA meetings. The Massachusetts Housing Partnership has given technical assistance to 85 mostly small local governments to help them review proposed projects.

Program Effectiveness/Units Built

Since the statute's inception in 1969, almost 30,000 housing units have been built in over 200 local jurisdictions. Since many developments are mixed income, approximately 22,000 units are reserved for households earning 80 percent of the AMI or less. Approximately 34 percent of all affordable units in the commonwealth of Massachusetts were constructed under Chapter 40B regulations.

Despite the program's success, the state remains below its stated goal of each community having 10 percent of the housing stock priced to be affordable. Of Massachusetts's 351 local jurisdictions, only 31 have a housing stock with 10 percent or more affordable units. Boston

and many of its suburbs exceed the 10 percent threshold. Two hundred thirty communities have less than 5 percent affordable housing. There are many reasons why a community may have a low rate of affordable units: small lots that make mixed-income development impossible, high land values or no available land, and low demand for affordable housing.

Chapter 40B has had the indirect effect of stimulating the creation of housing programs at the local level. The most successful communities promote the construction of affordable housing, often without the need to invoke Chapter 40B. When a local government implements a housing program or reaches the goal of 10 percent affordable housing, it retains control over the makeup of its housing stock.

In terms of Chapter 40B's effectiveness in providing affordable housing for individuals, the program has been a success. Individuals are finding inexpensive housing in areas previously thought to be too expensive or too egalitarian. Low-cost housing remains difficult to find in some areas of the state, particularly dense urban areas.

The selection of residents varies from project to project, as there is no state oversight of the affordability controls or target population once it is determined to meet Chapter 40B standards. The affordability controls vary according to the financing and subsidy programs used to develop them.

Challenges—Present and Future

Multifamily housing continues to be difficult to permit in Massachusetts, and Chapter 40B is effectively the only tool to create it in many localities. Massachusetts ranks 47th out of the 50 states in the number of multifamily permits built since 1990. Since affordable rental housing is only practically available in multifamily settings, the supply of rental units lags behind the supply of owned units.

One challenge created by Chapter 40B has been the volume of comprehensive permit requests. Two-thirds are settled at the local level; however, the remaining third are appealed to the commonwealth's Housing Appeals

Committee. This has created a significant backlog of cases that must be mediated and ruled on by the five-member committee.

The challenge for towns across Massachusetts will continue to be reaching the 10 percent threshold of affordable housing. Chapter 40B is a powerful tool, especially when developments are considered "friendly." Friendly Chapter 40B developments could help many towns get affordable housing programs started. The fear of adversarial Chapter 40B proposals creates an incentive for towns with little or no affordable housing to create programs and plans under local control.

The sustainability of affordable housing under Chapter 40B is quite good. Unlike inclusionary zoning programs, Chapter 40B can continue to produce housing when available land is built out. Nonprofit and limited partnership developers can place infill housing on parcels of their choice. As available land becomes increasingly scarce and housing prices rise, Chapter 40B is likely to be an important component of the affordable housing system in Massachusetts.

The Chapter 40B Task Force

In February 2003, Massachusetts Governor Mitt Romney created a task force to conduct a comprehensive review of the Chapter 40B law to evaluate the statute and its impact and to ensure that the need to create affordable rental and for-sale housing is balanced appropriately with other municipal concerns. The task force was composed of members of the legislature, state housing officials, municipal and regional officials, and stakeholders representing development and environmental issues.

Part of the impetus for the task force was numerous bills filed with the legislature that would significantly weaken or repeal Chapter 40B. The governor requested delaying those bills until the task force made its recommendations to improve the law and its implementation. The task force made its findings and recommendations on May 30, 2003.

The task force found that while only 31 of Massachusetts's 351 communities have reached their goal of having 10 percent of their housing affordable, they believe the affordability problem would be even worse today had the law not been enacted. They stated that "without this powerful and innovative tool to create affordable housing, the affordability crisis in Massachusetts would be exacerbated." They refer to the law as the "most powerful state subsidy" available to build affordable housing in the commonwealth. They go on to clarify that by "subsidy" they mean "incentive" and not a budgetary outlay. Most housing built under Chapter 40B is developed without any monetary subsidy from the state.

While the task force was generally supportive of the law, they did issue a series of recommendations that they believed would improve the effectiveness of the law. They recommended creating incentives to make new Chapter 40B developments consistent with smart growth principles including sustainable development, development in areas with existing infrastructure, and location near public transportation. The full report, including all task force recommendations, can be accessed at http://www.state.ma.us/dhcd/Ch40Btf.

Case Studies:

Successful Developments

Stapleton: Denver, Colorado

The closing of Denver's Stapleton International Airport to make way for the new airport created one of the largest pieces of urban land available for redevelopment in the United States. The city of Denver seized the opportunity to create a sustainable new urbanist community with 10 percent of the housing reserved for low- and moderate-income families. The scale of the project has brought about a partnership with the developer and the Denver school representatives.

STAPLETON FACTS

Land Use: Total area of 7.5 square miles. Eight thousand owner-occupied dwelling units, 4,000 rental units. Ten million square feet of office space, 3 million square feet of retail space. One thousand one hundred acres of open space and trails.

Affordability: Approximately 800 for-sale homes and 800 apartments at Stapleton have been or will be built under a workforce housing program. Ten percent of total housing stock is designated as affordable.

FUNDING/PROGRAMS

Funding: Fannie Mae's American Communities Fund, tax-exempt bond issue, Low Income Housing Tax Credits (LIHTCs), tax increment financing (TIF).

Programs: Discounted land sale from developer, public/private partnership.

Developer: Forest City Stapleton, Inc. (Denver, Colorado).

Architects: Multiple.

General Description

The Stapleton project is a mixed-use, master-planned community currently under construction on the former site of Denver's Stapleton International Airport. At 7.5 square miles (4,700 acres), it is the largest urban infill project in the nation's history. The project is scheduled for completion in 2020 at a cost nearly $4 billion. The site will accommodate 8,000 owned dwelling units, 4,000 rental units, 10 million square feet of office space, and 3 million square feet of retail space.

Stapleton's master planners and developers paid close attention to progressive, sustainable issues such as "green"[17] building development and workforce housing. The sheer size of Stapleton and the diversity of employment within necessitate a focus on workforce housing to ensure that service workers, teachers, and law enforcement officers can afford to live near their place of employment. Eight hundred owner-occupied homes are planned, along with several hundred apartments. As of the writing of this book, approximately 10 percent of all affordable dwelling units are constructed and occupied. All developers in Stapleton must agree to build according to the standards of the Home Builders Association of Metro Denver for energy efficiency, healthy indoor air, reduced water usage, and preservation of natural resources.

Development Process

In November 1995, the Denver Urban Redevelopment Authority signed a cooperative agreement with the city to form the Stapleton Development Corporation (SDC). The SDC was created as a vehicle for the dispersal of property. The SDC also funded a study that found the Stapleton area to be "blighted," thereby clearing the way for its designation as an urban renewal area and making it eligible for tax increment financing (TIF). TIF eligibility allowed bonds to be issued, and the debt to be serviced by the increase in property taxes collected when property values rise.

Stapleton Development Corporation chose Forest City Enterprises as the master developer. Forest City agreed to buy the land from the city and county of Denver over time, so as to eliminate the costs and risks associated with having to hold the land. Forest City agreed to pay $79.4 million over a 15-year period for 2,935 acres. Forest City is also responsible for constructing local infrastructure. The developer advanced the front-end financing for regional infrastructure through a $30 million TIF. Forest City bought its first land in 2001, and agreed to buy 1,000 acres every five years through 2015.

Forest City worked closely with Denver Public Schools to negotiate the establishment of new public schools in Stapleton. The developer felt strongly that good neigh-

borhood schools would be a powerful attractor for potential residents, and absolutely necessary to attract middle-class residents back to the city. They hoped to appeal to homeowners who are looking for a "third choice" in where they live. Currently, residents must choose between old homes in the city and new homes in the suburbs. Stapleton provides the access to jobs and connectivity of the urban area but offers the greenery, parks, and good schools often found in the suburbs.

Forest City donated ten acres of land and $500,000 for the Denver School of Science and Technology (DSST), the first public charter high school to be constructed at Stapleton. The school will be dedicated to proficiency in math, science, and technology and it has been selected as one of the Bill and Melinda Gates Foundation's national demonstration project schools.

(Left) Forest City Stapleton is constructing a mixed-use, master-planned community on 7.5 square miles of land on the former site of Stapleton International Airport in Denver.

Stapleton is also home to a regular public elementary school and a public charter elementary school under one roof, sharing common facilities and play areas. The joint campus opened in August 2003. The charter school, known as the Odyssey School, is an Expeditionary Learning school modeled after the Outward Bound program. The expeditionary learning school model design is one of seven "break the mold" school designs funded over a five-year period by New American Schools, a Bush Administration and private sector initiative that calls for radically new models of education built upon high standards and yielding dramatic improvement in student achievement. There are now more than 50 Expeditionary Learning schools in 14 places nationwide.

Financing and Programs

Stapleton is a public/private partnership. The ability to create TIF from the project is key to funding the $600 million in local and regional infrastructure costs. In order to accomplish this, the Denver Urban Redevelopment Authority (DURA) became involved in the Stapleton redevelopment effort in 1995. Since DURA is the only entity in Denver with the statutory power to fund

(Below) Clyburn at Stapleton provides 100 units of affordable housing to income-qualified senior citizens.

redevelopment through the use of TIF, its involvement has been necessary to help finance the project. The TIF increment yielded $835,000 in 2001.

Forest City purchased $145 million in bonds from the Park Creek Metropolitan District to underwrite the initial infrastructure required for the redevelopment. Forest City also secured a $25 million loan from National City Bank for the initial land purchase.

Affordable housing at Stapleton has, so far, been financed in part by Fannie Mae's American Communities Fund, and Low Income Housing Tax Credits assisted by discounted land costs. Housing affordability is a serious problem in Denver—a family needs to earn approximately $65,000 in order to afford the median-priced home, assuming good credit and availability of down-payment funds. Approximately 56 percent of Denver families earned less than $50,000 in 2000.

Planning and Design

Conceived as a sustainable community, Stapleton was meant to integrate jobs, housing, and the environment. In order to create a vision for such a large undertaking, the city and county of Denver entered into a partnership agreement with the Stapleton Redevelopment Foundation (SRF) in 1991. The SRF is a nonprofit 501(c)(3) corporation established by community leaders to maximize the opportunities within Stapleton. Together with the city, they raised over $4 million to create the Stapleton Redevelopment Plan or "Green Book," which was completed and approved in 1995.

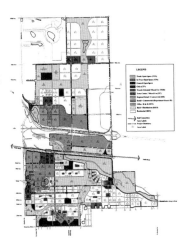

(Right) The higher-density new urbanist master plan for Stapleton allows for the significant preservation of usable connected open space.

The Green Book outlines a clear dedication to affordable housing, traditional neighborhood design, environmental conservation, and high-quality educational opportunities. Stapleton will mirror the design of surrounding communities, with front porches, modest lot sizes, pocket parks, and narrow neighborhood streets. Stapleton is based on traditional neighborhood design principles and provides physical and economic connections to the surrounding neighborhood. Fortifying the green philosophy is the requirement that builders must meet or exceed the "Built Green" standards of the Home Builders Association of Metro Denver, which encourages energy efficiency, healthy indoor air, reduced water usage, and the preservation of natural resources.

The Green Book divides Stapleton into seven planning districts and contains plans for five mixed-use town centers. Comprising office and retail uses, the town centers are designed to be within walking distance of most residential areas. "Neighborhoods" measuring 100 acres in size are spaced around the town centers.

Affordability and Management/Marketing

Ten percent, or approximately 800, of the single-family homes sold at Stapleton will be built under the Home-Buyer Resource Program. The program was designed to put housing within reach of teachers, nurses, police officers, and other members of the community's workforce. Forest City dedicated itself to establishing a comprehensive affordable housing program and created the Associate Developer Program to work with local nonprofit housing agencies and small development firms that wanted to build affordable housing within Stapleton. Forest City provides technical expertise and guidance to the developers chosen, many of whom do not have experience with the scale or deed limitations associated with the project.

The Stapleton affordable housing program specifies that the affordable units must be developed in mixed-income areas and adhere to minimum square footage guidelines. For example, a studio apartment cannot be smaller than 400 square feet and a three-bedroom unit cannot be smaller than 1,100 square feet. At least 15 percent of the units must have three or more bedrooms. The associate developers and Forest City must report to the SDC their progress in fulfilling the affordable housing requirements.

To be eligible to purchase one of the affordable homes, a buyer must have a gross household income below specific target amounts published annually by the U.S. Department of Housing and Urban Development (HUD). In order to ensure long-term affordability for future homebuyers, 30-year resale price restrictions will apply to the homes. At the end of 30 years, a nonprofit entity created to control and monitor the for-sale units has the option of A) buying back the homes at restricted prices and reselling them at a new restricted price, or B) letting them be sold on the open market and collecting the difference, to be spent on other affordable housing programs in the area. The owner gets to keep a share of the appreciation depending on how long he or she has been in the residence.

For example, in 2003 a HomeBuyer home was sold for $140,000, which is $20,000 less than its market value. When the property is sold in 2033, its market value is $200,000. The $60,000 of appreciation is split evenly between the nonprofit entity and the seller. If the seller lives in the home for less than 30 years, the appreciation taken by the seller is prorated. The seller does not realize the full profit of the sale, but he or she did buy the unit below market rate, with minimal associated costs and an excellent location. The house remains below market rate after the sale, and a second buyer can purchase it.

The 80-unit Roslyn Court is the first affordable housing development built at Stapleton. One-, two-, and three-bedroom homes priced from the $120,000s to $175,000 are currently being sold. Units are fairly small, measuring only 600 square feet for one-bedroom homes and 1,100 square feet for three-bedroom residences. Syracuse Village, the second affordable housing project, consists of condominiums and townhomes ranging in size from 788 to 1,155 square feet. Prices start in the mid-$100,000s. Both are available to those earning 80 percent or less of the area median income, which is $55,900 for a family of four. Buyers are expected to contribute 3 to 5 percent of the purchase price, work at least 30 hours a week unless over 62 years of age, and agree to owner-occupy the resi-

dence. Buyers must also attend an orientation and a homebuyer education class.

The first rental project is Clyburn at Stapleton, a 100-unit affordable apartment community for residents over 62 years of age. Located adjacent to a town center, it is equipped with laundry, computer, and community rooms. Monthly rents range from $710 for a one-bedroom unit up to $890 for a two-bedroom apartment. Income limits and rents are based on HUD's annual income limits, which in 2003 was $33,500 for a two-person household. Mercy Housing Southwest has built 69 low-income rental apartments on a two-acre site donated by Forest City. Mercy Housing's community is set to open in 2005. The community leased up in 2005.

Because construction has not begun on most of the site, it is important to market both the existing and planned developments in Stapleton. The Forest City Stapleton Visitor Center welcomes visitors, buyers, renters, and business owners to the area. The center features a video wall that integrates actual aerial footage with "virtual reality" images of neighborhoods to be built. A network of "pavilions" offers a glimpse into the residential, office, and retail space of the new mixed-use neighborhoods. The pavilions also provide information about Stapleton initiatives such as sustainable development, traditional neighborhood design, and mixed use.

Lessons Learned

■ Controlled reselling of affordable homes keeps them within reach of moderate-income people in perpetuity. The first owners gain financially, but pass on an affordable home upon resale.

■ Affordable housing can be incorporated into a project of much larger scope. Advance planning is needed to include mixed-income housing into the master plan.

Casa del Maestro: Santa Clara, California

With some of the most expensive housing in the country, Santa Clara County has difficulties attracting and retaining teachers. The Santa Clara Unified School District directly addressed this problem by building 40 affordable apartments designated for teachers on surplus school property. Through innovative financing and partnership with a for-profit developer, this development stands out as a creative solution to a difficult problem.

> **CASA DEL MAESTRO FACTS**
> **Land Use:** 2.16 acres of garden-style apartments.
> Affordability: Forty units of below-market-rate rental apartments. All residents must be teachers working in the Santa Clara Unified School District. Rents are estimated to be 50 percent of the prevailing market rate.
>
> **FUNDING/PROGRAMS**
> **Funding:** Certificates of Participation (COP), land dedication.
> **Programs:** Nonprofit rental property management.
> **Developer:** Thompson Residential (Sausalito, California).
> **Architect:** KTGY Group (Irvine, California).

General Description

Casa del Maestro (literally translated as "house of the teacher") is a 40-unit apartment complex rented exclusively to teachers in the Santa Clara Unified School District. The school district built and owns the complex to provide affordable housing to its teachers, who are particularly vulnerable to housing shortages.

California's Silicon Valley faces a serious crisis of affordable housing. During the late 1990s, when technology companies were expanding in earnest, median for-sale home prices shot past $500,000. Rents for properties also rose substantially, with an average two-bedroom apartment costing over $2,000 per month. Even after the technology boom market ended, prices remained

high. Home prices and rents—particularly for new properties—remained out of reach for much of the region's workforce. Skilled public service professionals like firefighters, nurses, and teachers were not able to find suitable housing within Santa Clara County.

For the Santa Clara Unified School District, attracting and retaining high-quality teachers was and still is a challenge. It is difficult to attract teachers to a district where housing is so expensive, which in turn leads to a high rate of turnover. In the late 1990s, the school district was experiencing five-year teacher attrition rates of over 300 percent. Leadership within the district determined that the cost of attrition was higher than the cost of providing affordable housing to teachers.

Development Process

The school district owned a 2.16-acre surplus site adjacent to an existing school, which was dedicated as the site of Casa del Maestro. Owning the land was a huge factor in keeping development costs down and keeping the apartments affordable. The surrounding neighborhood was developed during the 1950s and was low-rise suburban in character. While the local housing stock is modest in scale, values are quite high. Scattered throughout the neighborhood are a number of small, two-story apartment complexes that served as a design guide for the developer of the subject property.

The developer of Casa del Maestro was Sausalito-based Thompson Residential, a regional provider of luxury housing that has created some of the San Francisco Bay Area's most successful upscale rental and condominium communities. Thompson Residential's involvement was a twist on the "double bottom line" approach to community-sensitive development efforts. The developer trades a lower return for the satisfaction and public acknowledgment of having provided a community service in the form of affordable housing. Thompson proposed to act as the project developer in return for reimbursement of costs including in-house project management, but no additional fees or profit. The primary "return" would be strengthened relations with the Santa Clara Unified School District and the city and county of Santa Clara. Thompson plans to pursue for-profit development opportunities in that area in the near future.

The project was bid by Thompson to a general contractor, with ground breaking in April 2001. After completion of construction and issuance of a certificate of occupancy, the district took possession of Casa del Maestro in May 2002. Construction was completed on time (two years) and under budget.

Financing and Programs

The school district also enjoyed political goodwill and citizen support. However, the district had substantial debt service obligations, and putting another bond issue on the ballot could further delay the project's completion. The decision was made to pursue certificate of participation (COP) financing.

The California School Boards Association (CSBA) Finance Corporation assists school districts throughout California in institutional fiscal matters. The CSBA helps districts finance renovations, operates lend/lease programs for large items, and invests cash reserves. The COP program allows school districts to finance capital improvement projects with little or no downpayment and favorable interest rates. COPs can fund new buildings, buses, athletic facilities, or major renovations. Over the life of the program, COPs have funded 135 projects worth over $623 million statewide. The repayment for making capital improvements is structured with a lessor-lessee contract. Since the school district is not technically taking on debt, public referenda are not needed. This makes certificates of participation more advantageous than issuing bonds. The school district argued that housing for teachers was as critical an infrastructure need as school buses, athletic fields, or portable classrooms. By qualifying the housing project as an infrastructure need, it became eligible for COP financing.

Casa del Maestro translates as "House of the Teacher." The community was designed to appeal to the relatively sophisticated tastes and desires of the target audience of schoolteachers.

Planning and Design

The Casa del Maestro site had been used as a dog park for many years, and there was some modest resistance to losing it. In general, however, the neighborhood was highly supportive of the development effort. The site lies within walking distance of neighborhood-serving retail and offers convenient freeway access. The area is served by CalTrain commuter rail, although the station is not within walking distance.

All 40 units were constructed in a horseshoe formation that allowed for single-car garage parking for most units. Sloped roofs created covered patios on the street side, while the rear of each unit faces green open space. Units are accessed directly from the street to reinforce the townhouse feel of the property. The complex was designed with Victorian exteriors, mimicking San Francisco's Presidio district with white-on-white siding and red shingle roofs. In order to blend in with the surrounding neighborhood, the buildings were constructed with a low profile and decorative end units that resemble a single-family house facade.

Efforts were made to maintain the affordability of the apartments while also creating an attractive, livable space. The district and the developer recognized that teachers are seeking a high quality of life from their homes. The 24 one-bedroom and 16 two-bedroom units feature a washer and dryer, patios, and views of open space. Seventy percent of units have direct-access garages. The complex also features a community room and a swimming pool. Thompson Residential resisted the temptation to make the units smaller. Instead, some interior amenities that are standard in market-rate units—such as granite countertops, upgraded appliances, and elaborate light fixtures—were bypassed in favor of cheaper options to hold down the total development cost.

Affordability and Management/Marketing

A nonprofit foundation was formed to administer and manage Casa del Maestro. This allowed the Santa Clara Unified School District to control the future of the property while keeping tenants—who are all district employees—at "arm's length." The rental contract is contingent upon employment with the school district, and the maximum length of time tenants are allowed to live in the complex is five years. Within the five-year time frame, it is hoped that teachers will be able to build a nest egg and purchase a home. Homebuyer assistance and education programs are provided through the city government.

The response to this housing opportunity was overwhelming, and the district instituted a lottery to ensure that future residents were chosen fairly. Information about the housing program and guidelines for entering the process were distributed to school employees by the

The community clubhouse at Casa del Maestro is heavily used for parties and gatherings.

district. To qualify, employees had to have worked for the district for less than three years, with priority given to teachers first, administrators second, and certified employees third. There has been a varied mix of renters, including families, couples, and singles.

Rents were set at the minimum amount that would be required to cover actual operating costs, debt service on the underlying bond financing, and a small sink fund. This resulted in rental rates for one-bedroom units of $650 to $730, about half of the regional average rent. The one-bedroom units represented a unique opportunity for young teachers newly out of college to avoid the roommate situations that are common in high-cost locales.

Teachers living in Casa del Maestro have responded very well to their new home. Most report an enjoyable experience living in a community of teachers, which gives them an informal support network. Young teachers are staying on the job longer and report more job satisfaction. The district has plans to build more rent-controlled housing for teachers.

Lessons Learned

■ Land dedication by the Santa Clara Unified School District was crucial to building a below-market-rate housing complex. Many municipalities, school districts, and other agencies have surplus parcels of land that could be developed as affordable housing.

■ Constituent group housing needs a visible, respected champion to build community consensus and political will.

■ Other government service workers such as police officers, firefighters, and municipal employees could also benefit from constituent group housing. In areas where housing markets are tight, these important members of the community could be priced out of living in the jurisdictions they serve. This results in long commutes, less productive workers, and high rates of turnover.

■ Professional workforce housing must replicate the amenities, location, and quality of market-rate housing. Highly trained professionals demand a high quality of life from their homes.

■ In cases where an agency owns housing that is rented to its employees, a third-party property manager should handle the leasing and upkeep of the property. This keeps the owner/employer at an "arm's length" from the tenant/employee.

(Above) Every apartment at Casa del Maestro looks out onto open space.

(Right) Two mature palm trees were planted as part of a generous landscaping plan that gave the community a sense of sophistication and permanence.

Edgemoore at Carrington: McLean, Virginia

As required by the Fairfax County Affordable Dwelling Unit Ordinance, eight units in this luxury suburban community were designated as affordable. The affordable townhouse units were integrated into the single-family detached community by constructing them to look like the surrounding single-family homes. No public subsidy was required.

> ## EDGEMOORE AT CARRINGTON FACTS
> **Land Use:** Eight affordable units constructed as part of a 105-unit subdivision with 97 luxury single-family detached residences and eight affordable townhouses built in the "great house" design to resemble two large single-family homes.
> **Affordability:** Eight of the units are reserved for individuals or families earning at or below 70 percent of the area median income for the Washington, D.C., Standard Metropolitan Statistical Area.
>
> ## FUNDING/PROGRAMS
> **Funding:** Private financing sources and developer equity.
> **Programs:** Fairfax County Affordable Dwelling Unit Ordinance.
> **Developer:** Edgemoore Homes (Vienna, Virginia).
> **Architect:** Custom Design Concepts Architecture (McLean, Virginia).

General Description

The Carrington development, located near the office and shopping destination of Tysons Corner (about 13 miles west of Washington, D.C.), contains county-mandated affordable housing units that blend in with the surrounding luxury homes, which now sell for over $1 million. This is achieved through an architectural illusion known as a "great house," which is designed to look like a large, single-family detached home but actually contains four townhouse units, each with its own front entrance and garage parking. This type of design provides more uniformity in a development of large single-family residences. Previously, Fairfax County developers with Affordable Dwelling Unit (ADU) requirements had built only townhouse or low-rise multifamily construction, which tended to stand out, and often apart, from the market-rate units offered elsewhere in the development.

The developer, Edgemoore Homes, planned Carrington as a luxury enclave in McLean, Virginia, an affluent suburb of Washington, D.C. The project contains 105 units—eight affordable units and 97 market-rate units. The market-rate units measure about 4,000 to 5,000 square feet and are located on half-acre lots. The site is further advantaged by proximity to a major state highway (Route 7) and the Dulles Toll Road (which provides easy access to Dulles International Airport and neighboring business corridors). The parcel, a relatively flat piece of land 70 acres in size, was a former dairy farm whose owners had resisted selling until the early 1990s, when they sold it to Edgemoore Homes. The site is bordered on the west by the Wolf Trap Woods subdivision, which comprises medium-sized single-family homes built during the mid-1970s.

While not providing a large amount of affordable housing, the Fairfax County Affordable Dwelling Unit ordinance does achieve several county goals. Being an inclusionary zoning program, the ADU ordinance distributes affordable housing across new residential developments throughout the county, rather than concentrating it in lower-income neighborhoods as past programs had. The geographic dispersion of the affordable housing allows low- and moderate-income families access to high-quality county services, including some of the best public schools in the country. In addition, the units are constructed by the private sector, requiring no public subsidy, outside of administrative program costs.

Development Process

The site was originally zoned R-1, meaning one dwelling unit per acre, which allowed for 70 units. The Edgemoore development team decided to increase density and asked the county for a zoning change to R-2. This allowed them to build close to 100 units—their ideal number of units for the project. The zoning request for increased density, combined with the fact that the development would yield more than 50 units, automatically required the project to heed Fairfax County's Affordable Dwelling Unit Ordinance. Edgemoore Homes was now required to provide units that could be afforded by those earning low to moderate incomes. The number of market-rate units and density determined the final amount of units. Carrington developers built 8 percent as ADUs.

The residents of the neighboring Wolf Trap Woods subdivision resisted the inclusion of affordable housing so close to their homes. Often, neighbors perceive below-market-rate projects as synonymous with public housing and its associated baggage—increased crime, litter, noise, and subsequently lower property values. As William Fischel stated in his book *The Homevoter Hypothesis*, homeowners will seek to protect their homes' values, which for many Americans is their biggest investment. Newspaper accounts of the controversy quote a Wolf Trap Woods resident as saying the ADUs should be banned from developments containing large, single-family homes and that the county should not "try to solve sociological problems by breaking the zoning."[18] Thus NIMBYism became an issue, and because the development plan needed the approval of the Wolf Trap Woods Homeowners Association in order to be approved for the density increase, it significantly slowed progress on the project. Edgemoore Homes made it clear to the Wolf Trap Woods residents that they would be building traditional townhomes, as Fairfax County had typically approved for ADUs (along with multifamily). However, the homeowners association did not approve of the townhomes, claiming that their nonconforming appearance would clash with that of the established large, detached single-family homes.

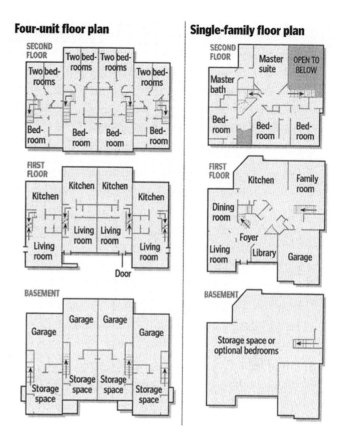

Carrington floor plans. The townhouse units average 1,200 square feet in size, compared with 4,000 to 5,000 square feet for the single-family detached market-rate homes.

In previous developments in Fairfax County where affordable housing had been required, the townhomes stand alone, often at the edge of the development and far removed from the detached single-family homes. It would be obvious to someone driving around one of these developments that the affordable housing was segregated and designed differently from the market-rate housing. Not only was this approach unacceptable to those living near the Carrington project, but it also made it difficult to sell to those wanting to buy in the development. Developers discovered that few people wanted to buy a $500,000 house next to a $120,000 townhouse.

Financing and Programs

Because this was a luxury single-family home development and density increases were granted to account for the addition of the affordable units, no public financing was required. The project was financed through private financing sources combined with developer equity. The affordable units were provided as a result of the Fairfax County Affordable Dwelling Unit Ordinance.

Fairfax County, Virginia, a suburb of Washington, D.C., is one of the most affluent counties in the United States. As of 2003, the median family income in the county was $93,000 and the median cost of a single-family home was $380,000. In order to afford such a house, a family of four would have to earn about $109,000 a year, but 53 percent of the county's families earn below that amount. Fairfax County, long aware of this discrepancy, has worked to find an amenable solution through its Affordable Dwelling Unit ordinance.

In 1971, Fairfax County passed a mandatory zoning ordinance that required that developers of more than 50 multifamily dwelling units provide 15 percent of their units to those earning between 60 and 80 percent of area median income. The Virginia Supreme Court overturned this ordinance requirement in 1973 on the grounds that it involved a "taking," or surrendering property rights without just compensation (*Board of Supervisors of Fairfax County et al.* v. *DeGroff*). Fifteen years later, a local affordable housing advocacy group called AHOME (Affordable Housing Opportunity Means Everyone) worked at the state and local levels to lobby for acceptance of an affordable housing ordinance. Because Virginia is a "Dillon's Rule" state, Fairfax County could not devise the ordinance on its own. Local planning and zoning authority had to be granted to the locality by the state legislature in Richmond. AHOME not only had to convince local politicians, but also had to work with state lawmakers to amend state-enabling legislation to allow jurisdictions the right to pass inclusionary zoning ordinances. In 1989, Virginia amended its state code to allow localities to adopt such ordinances and the Fairfax County measure was enacted in 1990. In order to prevent the Affordable Dwelling Unit measure from being deemed a taking, developers are granted a density bonus.

This multifamily building houses four affordable townhomes; the exterior appearance, however, blends with the large luxury single-family homes in the surrounding community.

The ordinance applies to developments of 50 units or more seeking to increase density above an R-1 designation. (Developments with fewer than 50 units and/or not seeking to increase density are not required to build affordable units, but the developers are required to donate 0.5 percent of the each unit's estimated sales price to the county's affordable housing trust fund.) Developments containing single-family homes receive a 20 percent density bonus, but they are required to build 12.5 percent of the total as affordable units (the percentage can decrease depending on proffers or mitigating circumstances). For nonelevator, multifamily buildings or elevator multifamily buildings fewer than four stories high, a 10 percent density bonus is allowed and up to 6.25 percent of all units are to be designated as affordable. Fairfax County had excluded multifamily buildings of four stories or more with at least one elevator, but in 2003 the county board of supervisors voted to include mid-rise development in the ordinance. In order to accomplish this in mid-rise developments, the regulations offer up to 17 percent density bonuses in exchange for up to 6.25 percent ADUs. Developments that have 50 percent structured parking will be required to provide only up to 5 percent ADUs.

Fairfax County affordable housing activists continue to lobby for increases in the percentage of affordable housing units in each development. As of 2003, Fairfax County had 1,436 affordable units, despite the fact that the ordinance has been in place for close to 15 years. The program was not immediately popular with developers who claimed loss of profit and slowdowns due to NIMBYism ("Not In My Back Yard"). Developers can appeal the ADU requirement, but the county rarely makes exceptions. Circumstances such as infeasibility or proffers can decrease an ADU requirement, but not dismiss it. Over the past decade, the ordinance has been amended to ease the burden on developers and builders. Developers are now allowed to slightly increase their sales prices in exchange for using a sympathetic design (such as the great house) or to cover the costs of enhancing the appearance of the units. In 1998, the ordinance was amended to allow developers to complete up to 90 per-

cent of the market-rate units upon completion of 90 percent of the required ADUs. Previously, developers could not complete more than 75 percent of the market-rate units before completing 100 percent of the ADUs. The county provides developers with guidelines for the construction of the units to ensure appropriate square footage and amenities.

Planning and Design

In response to this dilemma, architects at the McLean, Virginia, firm Custom Design Concepts Architecture developed the great-house design. (The great-house duplex design had been used in previous projects in Fairfax County, but Carrington was the first project to use the "multiplex" model.) By disguising the townhouses as a large, single-family house compatible with the market-rate unit designs being offered by Edgemoore, potential neighbors inside and outside the development could be satisfied. According to Carrington's developers, the great-house design eased NIMBY tensions and did not hinder sales of units within the development.

The great-house design also seems to appeal to those purchasing the units. Carrington offered eight affordable units split between two great houses. The first eight families who were eligible to buy the affordable units at Carrington bought them immediately, which, according to the developer, is unusual with Fairfax ADUs. Some potential buyers do not like the location or the design of an available unit and will elect to remain on Fairfax County's ADU waiting list. The developer credited the exterior design, garage space, and large bedrooms as part of the Carrington ADUs' appeal. Residents include schoolteachers, taxicab drivers, a waiter, and a Fairfax County tollbooth collector.

Although Carrington's great houses were the first of their kind in Fairfax County, constructing them did not present any problems. The builder was able to put them up quickly, which was especially important, as the completion of the ADUs was necessary to obtain permits for the remaining market-rate units. Since the great houses typically do not have driveways, additional parking and garbage pickup areas are located behind the house and at a lower grade. Carrington's developers were also careful to integrate two great houses into the development and not isolate them from the other 97 market-rate residences. In fact, quite the contrary—the units were placed near the front of the development and are readily visible alongside the market-rate units as seen from the main roadway. Carrington's developers say that they did not encounter any difficulties obtaining financing for the project and that Fairfax County was amenable to their design suggestions. However, Fairfax County did dictate the minimum square footage, room size allotment, and type of amenities. The great-house style blends in with the English country manner design of the market-rate units.

Affordability and Management/Marketing

In order to qualify for a unit, a person or family must be earning at or below 70 percent of the area median income for the Washington, D.C., Standard Metropolitan Statistical Area, not owned a home in the past three years, and attend a course on homeownership. After they are approved, they are placed in lottery. Priority is given to those who live or work in Fairfax County or have children under 18 at home. The waiting list includes hundreds of names, and because not many units are produced in a given year, the county states that those not meeting the priority requirements most likely will not receive a unit.

The units remain under a restrictive covenant maintaining their affordability for 15 years. (Fairfax recently lowered the amount of time. Previously it was 50 years.) In exchange for receiving a price-reduced unit and in order to keep the unit affordable, the selling owners receive a small price appreciation per year that is linked to the Consumer Price Index. Owners are also given appreciation credit for improvements they have made to the unit. The county oversees the appraisal, pricing, and sale of the units. The county must also make sure that owners are not renting out their unit and discourage them from taking refinancing offers from predatory lenders. If a unit goes into foreclosure, the affordability covenant is null and void and it must be sold to the highest bidder.

Owners may sell at any time and one-half of the net gain goes into the county's affordable housing trust fund. In exchange for using the great-house design, the developers were allowed to sell the units for slightly more than the typical ADU townhouse. When the units went to market in 2002, they were selling for $125,000 each or about $10,000 more than the typical three-bedroom ADU. The $10,000 difference put the units out of reach of about 5 percent of the 329 people on the county's waiting list. To afford a great-house unit, a family of four would have to have an annual income of $39,000 or more. According to the county, raising the sales prices also quelled surrounding communities' anxieties over the affordable units—for the most part.

In the end, the project has given eight households a chance at homeownership in a county where the median single-family home price is $379,854 (2003) and the median townhouse price is $229,929 (2003). There has been little turnover in the units and the developer claims the families are enjoying them. ADU residents are required to join the Carrington Homeowners Association, which covers common-space maintenance and trash removal. The ADUs are under special covenants to cap appreciation and must remain affordable for 15 years. Fairfax County supervised the homeownership lottery and will oversee turnover sales in the development.

The great-house concept is a one way of settling the physical discrepancies between Carrington's 4,000- to 5,000-square-foot market-rate homes and the 1,200-square-foot ADUs. The approach has also managed to quell NIMBYism and outright rejection of affordable housing in one of the most affluent counties in the nation. As of 2003, two other projects in Fairfax County have used the great-house design for their ADUs.

Lessons Learned

■ The great-house design concept can make community acceptance of affordable housing easier.

■ The county supported the developer's willingness to try a new design for the affordable housing.

■ With enough attention to design details, housing for low- and moderate-income households can be effectively integrated into high-income neighborhoods.

■ The inclusion of affordable units does not necessarily adversely affect the marketing of the luxury homes and these households can live together harmoniously.

■ Expect community opposition to affordable housing that will delay the entitlement and development process.

■ Density bonuses permit a developer to build more houses than would otherwise be permitted in exchange for making some of the units affordable. The density bonuses allow affordable housing production without the outlay of public funds.

Noji Gardens: Seattle, Washington

Noji Gardens is a mixed-income community in Seattle that was able to reduce construction costs, and thus preserve affordability, through the use of modular construction techniques. The development highlights the savings that can be achieved by modular construction as well as the complexity of existing building codes.

> **NOJI GARDENS FACTS**
> **Land Use:** Seventy-five total single-family homes in detached, duplex, and townhouse configurations on 6.5 total acres.
> **Affordability:** Fifty-one percent of homes are reserved for households with incomes of 80 percent or less than the area median income of $43,000. The rest were not reserved for any income level; however, homes were priced below the true market rate.
>
> **FUNDING/PROGRAMS**
> **Funding:** Section 108 Community Development Block Grant float loans, sub-market-rate loans from the Fannie Mae Foundation and the National Community Development Initiative (NCDI).
> **Programs:** HUD/Manufactured Housing Institute Demonstration Project, tax abatement area, Community Revitalization Area (CRA) designation, buyer assistance program offered by developer.
> **Developer:** HomeSight (Seattle, Washington).
> **Architect:** John McLaren (Seattle, Washington).

General Description

Noji Gardens is a 75-unit development located four miles southeast of downtown Seattle, Washington. Completed in 2002, Noji Gardens utilized manufactured, modular components to build two-thirds of the homes on the 6.5-acre site. The infill site was intended to serve a range of household incomes. Two-, three-, and four-bedroom single-family detached homes ranging from 1,300 to 1,400 square feet were built near the periphery to help transition to the surrounding neighborhood. Twenty-four 1,000-square-foot, two-bedroom townhomes and 40 three-bedroom townhomes with 1,400 square feet are found at the center of the development.

Seattle enjoys a strong economy, but housing costs are relatively high there. Growth management legislation has led to increased land values. Regulatory and construction costs are also driving up the cost of housing. Low- to moderate-income families in the Seattle area have difficulty finding close-in affordable homes. Developers in the Seattle area tend to build homes for middle- to upper-income people because the profit margins allow them to recoup the local regulatory and construction expenses. The developer of Noji Gardens, HomeSight, is a nonprofit developer that has tackled this complex problem by building new homes on infill sites intended for moderate-income buyers.

Development Process

HomeSight, a 501(c)(3) nonprofit community development corporation, has been revitalizing neighborhoods through affordable housing ownership. Operating only in the greater Seattle area, HomeSight has partnered with neighborhood groups, corporations, and lenders to construct or rehabilitate over 265 homes since its founding in 1990. The development corporation has received several national and local awards for innovative design, land use, and organizational excellence. Beyond the construction process, HomeSight assists buyers by providing homeowner education, counseling, and loan assistance. HomeSight extends its counseling and loan assistance programs to any homebuyer in need.

The site was divided into 2,400- to 4,000-square-foot lots. Construction took place in three phases at a total cost of $13 million. To develop the site, HomeSight had to build and pay for critical infrastructure such as roads, curbs, and sidewalks. HomeSight also needed to upgrade the utility services, which added $1.7 million to the development expenses. To contain infrastructure costs, HomeSight built private driveways instead of public alleys. To assist, the city of Seattle implemented a "latecomer" policy that requires developers who build adjacent to Noji Gardens to reimburse HomeSight for utilizing infrastructure that HomeSight built and paid for.

After reviewing the site plan, the city's engineering department required more curb cuts than HomeSight planned, which necessitated a redesign. The department's slow responses further impeded the permit process. Certain HUD code requirements on fourplexes further delayed the process. In all, permitting delays added two years to the project's development. The resulting increased costs of labor and finance charges contributed almost 40 percent to the final cost of homes. The final price of homes ranged from $162,000 to $259,000, before any purchase assistance was applied.

Financing and Programs

Funding for Noji Gardens came from a variety of sources. In 1998, the city of Seattle provided HomeSight with a 2 percent Section 108 CDBG float loan for interim site acquisition. Another CDBG float loan, issued in 2000, was used to refinance the site purchase and finance the acquisition of the 42 modular homes. U.S. Bank, the National Community Development Initiative (NCDI), and the Fannie Mae Foundation provided construction loans at below-market interest rates.

Because Noji Gardens falls within a designated Community Revitalization Area, all buyers of homes funded with HUD block grants are eligible for special HUD/Federal Housing Administration financing terms that reduce the upfront costs and buyer qualifications. In addition, the development is within the city tax abatement area, so buyers purchasing a home in a fourplex or denser structure can defer property taxes on their homes for ten years. Fannie Mae and HUD (through its block grant program and a special-purpose grant for such assistance) provided downpayment assistance to qualifying families.

Over half of the homes at Noji Gardens are reserved for households with incomes below 80 percent of the area's median income.

Planning and Design

The modular homes built in Noji Gardens are very different from traditional manufactured or mobile homes. Their exterior appearance is similar to, and they meet or exceed all building and insurance requirements of, "stick built" homes. The key difference is that modular homes are mass produced in several sections at a factory, transported to the building site, and assembled. The cost of raw construction materials for building a modular home is actually higher than a stick-built home. This is because the manufactured sections are reinforced to be strong enough to withstand the rigors of transport to the homesite. However, the overall cost of constructing modular homes compares favorably to the cost of building stick-built ones.

The cost savings associated with modular homes come from other points in the construction process. Modular homes are less expensive to construct because they can be produced quickly and efficiently in the controlled environment of a factory, which is protected from weather damage and delays. Those factories employ a skilled and permanent workforce generating continuous, high-volume production.

The decision to build Noji Gardens with manufactured, modular homes contributed to substantially reduced construction costs. HUD and the Manufactured Hous-

ing Institute had previously conducted a joint demonstration project in Pittsburgh, Pennsylvania. HomeSight saw the successful demonstration and the enormous potential it held to save on construction costs. Construction time is far shorter for modular homes than for stick-built homes. A modular house can be fully constructed in one to two months, instead of five to six months for a traditionally built home.

Modular homes are likely to be an increasingly popular way to provide affordable housing. A modular home can be up to 15 percent cheaper to construct than a comparable stick-built one. The industry average cost for constructing a modular home is $60,000 (not including land costs). As contractors and suppliers become more familiar with modular housing, the cost is expected to drop even further.

All homes in Noji Gardens have front porches.

The developer of Noji Gardens estimates that construction costs were reduced by 15 percent through the use of modular construction.

For HomeSight and architect John McLaren, it was important for Noji Gardens to blend in with the character of the surrounding community of two-story, single-family homes. Further, Washington State's Growth Management Act required jurisdictions to promote affordable housing at all income levels. Two-story homes are not a requirement of the Growth Management Act, but as an agency that pioneers small-lot development, HomeSight sees two-story homes as a necessity in achieving a satisfactory amount of living space when building on small lots.

Though the industry had already begun to address the possibility of creating two-story modular homes, it took three years to develop the components to construct the homes at Noji Gardens. Marlette Homes, of Hermiston, Oregon, worked with HomeSight's deputy director Tony To, the city of Seattle, the State of Washington Department of Labor and Industry, and local contractors to create a two-story modular home. The models created through the collaboration cost about 15 percent less than a comparable stick-built home. Cost savings are expected to reach up to 30 percent once the process has been refined by experience.

Affordability and Management/Marketing

Little marketing was needed to sell the homes at Noji Gardens. HomeSight's goal in pricing Noji Gardens was to keep prices low enough so that people in the neighboring area could afford to live there. As required by the conditions of the CDBG loan, 51 percent of the homes are reserved for households with incomes of 80 percent or less of the area median household income ($43,000). The affordable homes were marketed to people in the HomeSight education and assistance program. HomeSight did not attempt to presell any of the larger homes. The market-rate homes were listed with a real estate agent. All homes were sold within 90 days of completion.

Lessons Learned

Noji Gardens rendered several important lessons for workforce housing developers and policy makers, including:

■ Modular housing can be an effective building method for developers of affordable homes. Modular homes can be manufactured to look similar to stick-built homes, and to meet or exceed building standards.

■ Modular homes are cheaper to construct than stick-built homes. Savings in construction costs can be passed along to the buyer, making the unit more affordable.

■ Homebuyer education and training can help renters make the transition to homeownership. When the developer offers such programs, both the participant and the developer benefit. Participants are better equipped to buy a home, and the developer has a client base of informed and willing homebuyers.

■ HUD needs a more streamlined process to approve design changes. Substantial delays add unnecessarily to the final cost of homes.

Ohlone-Chynoweth Commons: San Jose, California

The Santa Clara Valley Transit Authority and Eden Housing have constructed affordable housing on the parking lot of an existing transit stop. The development provides much-needed affordable housing to the community as well as maximizes the public investment in the transit system by providing convenient transit access to a group that needs it the most, ensuring built-in ridership.

OHLONE-CHYNOWETH COMMONS FACTS

Land Use: One hundred ninety-four multifamily rental units, 4,400 square feet of retail, 4,000-square-foot community center, 369 surface parking spaces.

Affordability: All 194 units are reserved for families making between 30 and 60 percent of the region's median income (the U.S. Department of Housing and Urban Development set San Jose's median family income at $96,000 in 2002). Rents are set on a sliding scale according to income and unit size. One-bedroom units range from a minimum of $495 per month for a household earning 30 percent of the median income to $656 per month at 60 percent. Two-bedroom units range from $587 to $1,199; three-bedroom units rent for $678 to $1,383; and four-bedroom units run from $756 to $1,131. The pricing structure for the four-bedroom units represents an assumption that families needing these units will have decreased resources due to their large size.

FUNDING/PROGRAMS

Funding: Tax-exempt bonds, city of San Jose loan, Low-Income Housing Tax Credits, Metropolitan Transportation Commission grant, Federal Transit Administration Grant, Federal Home Loan Bank Grant, Proposition A funds.

Programs: Housing Initiative Program and Intensification Corridors Special Strategy, expedited application review, fee waivers.

Developer: Eden Housing, Inc. (Hayward, California).

Architect: Chris Lamen and Associates (San Rafael, California).

General Description

With average rents in San Jose peaking at $1,432 in 2002 (up almost 22 percent annually), housing affordability is a major issue in the city as well as in the surrounding region. Families are looking for places to live at ever-increasing distances from employment centers, and the impacts on the region's economy, traffic, and overall quality of life are enormous.

Meeting the needs of low-income families, Ohlone-Chynoweth Commons comprises housing and community facilities developed on an underused park-and-ride lot along the Guadalupe light-rail line. The former 1,100-space lot now accommodates diverse uses: 194 units of affordable housing, 4,400 square feet of retail uses, a 4,000-square-foot community center, and 369 parking spaces. Ohlone-Chynoweth Commons also features amenities attractive to moderate-income residents such as a child care center, a computer learning center, and a variety of recreational amenities—including tot lots and a bicycle/walking path. The development was undertaken as a joint development project between the Santa Clara Valley Transportation Authority (VTA) and Eden Housing, a nonprofit housing agency.

Eden Housing builds and maintains high-quality, well-managed, service-enhanced affordable community housing that meets the needs of lower-income families, seniors, and persons with disabilities. Since 1968, it has completed over 4,000 units of affordable housing in communities throughout northern California. Eden Housing provides property management and resident services through two affiliated nonprofit agencies.

Ohlone-Chynoweth Commons is part of the VTA's larger effort to integrate transportation and land use planning. The VTA actively pursues a number of projects as part of its strategic transit-oriented development (TOD) program. These include concept planning for many stations along the Tasman West light-rail line as well as three ambitious joint development projects that take advantage of underused park-and-ride lots while providing much-needed housing.

The VTA set a new precedent when it undertook what it refers to as a "trandominium" joint development project on the park-and-ride lot adjacent to the Ohlone-Chynoweth Station to develop Ohlone-Chynoweth Commons. Building affordable housing at or near transit stations has substantial benefits for both residents and the city. Residents will experience lower transportation costs and increased access to jobs due to the available transit line. The city and transit agency benefit from increased transit ridership and improved receipts from property taxes.

Development Process

Positioned along the 20-mile Guadalupe Rail Line at the Ohlone-Chynoweth Station, the site was identified as an ideal location for a joint development project for several reasons, including:

■ The Guadalupe line offered service to large and growing employment centers to the north.

■ The VTA had projected that future demand for the park-and-ride lot would leave significant available land that could be put to a higher use.

■ The owners of the adjacent site also were planning to develop multifamily housing, which would reinforce and support VTA's goals.

San Jose's Housing Initiative Program and Intensification Corridors Special Strategy, initiated in 1989 and approved by the city council in 1991, targeted station areas for high-density development around transit. This led to the creation of two designations: urban transit corridor residential (which provides for a minimum of 45 dwelling units per acre) and suburban transit corridor residential. The Ohlone-Chynoweth Station area was rezoned to suburban transit corridor residential, which allows for street-level commercial uses in residential developments and minimum densities of 20 dwelling units per acre .

Plans for Ohlone-Chynoweth Commons began in 1994. In 1995, the VTA chose nonprofit developer Eden Housing from among five proposals to develop the project. The development process was lengthy for several rea-

sons. First, although the city used an expedited process for application reviews, the number and types of issues raised by six homeowners' associations in the area caused the city council to defer decisions several times. Second, it was a fairly complicated process that involved many agencies and entities (including the VTA and multiple municipal and federal agencies). Finally, the VTA simply did not have the level of experience and staff needed to carry out a joint development process efficiently. Funding for the project came from a variety of sources (as described in more detail in the finance section), including federal grants as well as tax-exempt bonds and loans from the city. In particular, support from the city included funds to pay for the majority of fees and permits for the job as well as providing Eden with waivers for building and public works fees. This development was realized due to the commitment and cooperation of the VTA, the San Jose city planning and economic development agencies, the city council, Mayor Susan Hammer, and Eden Housing.

Financing and Programs

The total development cost for this project exceeded $30 million. The city issued $14.2 million in tax-exempt bonds, backed by a standby letter of credit from the Federal Home Loan Bank of San Francisco. The city also provided a $5.2 million loan as part of its efforts to support the development of affordable housing. Pacific Gas and Electric, now Union Bank, furnished $10.5 million in tax-credit equity for the project. The Metropolitan Transportation Commission gave a $574,000 grant (using urban mass transit funds) for landscaping and improvements to the station. The Federal Transit Administration provided a $250,000 grant to reconfigure the bus transfer center at the light-rail station. An additional $500,000 was given through an affordable housing grant from Federal Home Loan Bank and $350,000 was made available in State Proposition A funds to reimburse the school impact fee required for housing development.

Planning and Design

Ohlone-Chynoweth Commons consists of 194 mission-style apartments. Care was taken to integrate the project into the existing neighborhoods. The concerns of residents of surrounding neighborhoods—a predominantly middle-class community of single-family houses—focused on the lack of school capacity, increased traffic, and loss of taxpayer-built parking at the light-rail station. Also, with the addition of the project's 194 units to an adjacent 135 units of affordable housing built by Bridge Housing Corporation, neighbors were concerned about the impact of over 300 affordable housing units in one area. Numerous community meetings were held in response, which resulted in some design changes aimed at reducing the visual impact of the development.

The units closest to the existing neighborhood are of a townhouse style in four-unit blocks with garages, and are the least-dense units in the development. Toward the center of the development, and closer to the station, the building massing is much greater. With these changes, and with strong support from municipal agencies, the city council, and especially the mayor, the project was able to move forward.

In addition to design changes, the architects were challenged to find ways to maintain open space in a high-density development and to shelter outer-edge units from the noise generated by the highway and the light rail. Units face inward—toward landscaped pedestrian paths and a central lawn that serves as a small park—and away from traffic. Busy Chynoweth Avenue is buffered by large berms. Retail uses were placed along the south end of the project and adjacent to the light-rail station to protect residences from noise. Furthermore, exterior patios of outer units are lined with sound-resistant Plexiglas walls.

The apartments are built on top of podium (semi-recessed) parking, which is partially hidden by architectural details such as arched entryways and landscaping.

Ohlone-Chynoweth Commons consists of 194 mission-style apartments.

PHOTOGRAPH BY JAY GRAHAM, COURTESY OF CHRIS LAMEN & ASSOCIATES

Units are built back to back, with plumbing and electrical systems located in the common wall, lowering mechanical costs. Energy-efficient lighting and low-flow plumbing fixtures minimize tenants' water and electrical consumption.

Affordability and Management/Marketing

Ohlone-Chynoweth Commons is 100 percent affordable housing. It serves families with household incomes between 30 and 60 percent of the region's median income (the U.S. Department of Housing and Urban Development set San Jose's median family income at $96,000 in 2002), with rental prices set on a sliding scale according to income and unit size. One-bedroom units range from a minimum of $495 per month for a household earning 30 percent of the median income to $656 per month at 60 percent. Two-bedroom units range from $587 to $1,199; three-bedroom units go for $678 to $1,383; and four-bedroom units run from $756 to $1,131. The pricing structure for the four-bedroom units represents an assumption that families needing these units will have decreased resources due to their large size.

Because of the overwhelming demand for affordable housing in the region, very little marketing was needed to promote the development. Eden determined that little advertising was needed, listing the apartments only a few times in several local newspapers.

Approximately 5,000 families requested rental applications for the Commons. Of these, almost 2,000 applications were received. From all qualified applicants, 300 families were chosen by lottery to be interviewed for final qualification. Leasing began in November 2000 and the apartments were fully occupied by March 2001. Demand continues to be strong, and a waiting list is maintained for future tenants.

The 4,000 square feet (372 square meters) of retail space is 100 percent leased. A small grocery store takes up 1,500 square feet (139 square meters) and a florist, a coffee shop, and a hair salon occupy the remaining square footage. Eden Housing, which is responsible for leasing the retail as well as the residential portions of the development, reports that rents for the grocery market and other retail space average approximately $2 per square foot per month. Both Eden Housing and the VTA were concerned that because the retail was not visible from the street, it would not be a commercial success. There has not been as much demand for the retail services as initially anticipated, and the retail space eventually may become office space in the future.

PHOTOGRAPH BY JAY GRAHAM, COURTESY OF CHRIS LAMEN & ASSOCIATES

Open space was created in the interior of the community, away from the traffic surrounding the apartments.

Lessons Learned

■ From the VTA's point of view, the fiscal and legal challenges inherent in completing the joint development process were substantial and required significant proficiency in real estate development and property management. Although joint development is outside of a transit agency's core mission, the VTA staff considered the agency potentially well suited to spearhead such projects, as long as it owned the land. While a city planning agency's role is more "passive" (i.e., the agency zones the land but cannot choose who develops it), a transit agency has the opportunity to more actively direct the land development and, most important, to ensure that the land uses reinforce transit and vice versa. To do so successfully, however, requires a commitment to hire individuals with expertise.

■ The VTA has gained substantially from the development of Ohlone-Chynoweth Commons. Studies show that residents of TODs are up to five times more likely to commute by transit than residents who have to commute to the transit station. Ridership increases at the station since 2000 are in the double digits. The agency also receives a dedicated source of funding due to the ground lease, bringing in at least $250,000 each year for the next several decades. Both of these benefits were realized by simply developing a near-empty parking lot.

Developed on an underused park-and-ride lot, the Ohlone-Chynoweth Commons Apartments provide affordable housing and transit access to families in need of both.

PHOTOGRAPH BY JAY GRAHAM, COURTESY OF CHRIS LAMEN & ASSOCIATES

PHOTOGRAPH BY JAY GRAHAM, COURTESY OF CHRIS LAMEN & ASSOCIATES

Play areas were included in the interior community open space.

VTA staff members also offered the following observations learned while developing Ohlone-Chynoweth Commons:

■ Pay more attention to the program aspect of the project to ensure success of the retail uses, the child care center, and the computer space. For example, identify local businesses that would be particularly appropriate for the project and then offer them reduced rent for a period of time to assist them in getting established.

■ As the developer, Eden Housing believes that development would have been more efficient if the firm had been able to build fewer, yet taller buildings at a higher density ratio (current density is 27 units per acre). However, both the city and the neighbors limited the project's density and height.

Marshall Parkway: Marshall, Minnesota

Addressing continuing labor shortages, the Southwest Minnesota Housing Partnership joined with Schwan's Food Company (SWMHP), the major employer in the town of Marshall,l Minnesota, to develop affordable housing for company employees to encourage the retention of workers. The unique partnership included a significant financial contribution from Schwan's.

MARSHALL PARKWAY FACTS

Land Use: One hundred twenty units of mixed-income, single-family housing on 40 acres.

Affordability: Marshall Parkway consists of 82 single-family lots, three duplex lots, 18 moderate-income multifamily units, and 30 multifamily and mixed-income units ranging from 30 percent of statewide median income to market rate. Home-ownership was not restricted by income. The various funding mechanisms were available only to households meeting certain income thresholds. The permanent mortgage products had varying income requirements from 80 to 115 percent of the statewide median income. Gap and entry-cost assistance were income-restricted below 80 percent of the statewide median income. Rental housing is also available at market and affordable rates.

FUNDING/PROGRAMS

Funding: Tax increment financing, USDA Rural Redevelopment 502 Direct Loan program, USDA Rural Development Participation Loan Program, USDA Guaranteed Loan Program and single-family mortgage revenue bond permanent mortgage products. Zero-interest closing cost loans and grants, and market-rate first mortgage loans.

Programs: Major employer support and homebuyer education.

Developer: Southwest Minnesota Housing Partnership.

Architects: Cermak Rhodes Architects (St. Paul, Minnesota), and James Nelson McKellin III, Architect (Stillwater, Minnesota).

General Description

Marshall is located in rural southwest Minnesota, about 30 miles from the South Dakota state line and 150 miles from Minneapolis. With a population of 12,735, it is the largest city within a 100-mile radius. In the 1920s, food-processing industries began to grow in importance, and today are the leading economic activity there. Schwan's Food Company, the largest brand of frozen food in the United States, is headquartered in Marshall. With 2,500 employees in Marshall, Schwan's is the largest single employer in the city. Schwan's and all other major employers in Marshall reported labor shortages and problems recruiting and retaining necessary employees.

As part of their effort to create an area plan for the city, the Marshall Area Plan (MAP) committee was charged with developing goals relating to the future economic vitality and livability of the city. Through its analysis, the MAP committee identified the lack of affordable housing as a key barrier to sustainable economic development in Marshall. A subsequent study of housing needs confirmed the shortage of residential options. The studies found that the average sales price of housing units increased from $59,600 to $105,200 between 1990 and 1999. This represents an increase of 8 percent per year, significantly outpacing inflation and gains in income. The local workforce was being priced out of the market; 41 percent of Marshall's population earned less than $43,520, which is 80 percent of the statewide median income in 2000. Because of the region's rural nature, the profit margins of market-rate housing are very slim, leaving little room to price homes below market rate and make them affordable to low-income workers.

With the adoption of the MAP in 2000, the city realized that it had an affordable housing problem that was affecting its ability to compete economically.

Development Process

The Marshall Economic Development Agency (MEDA) began examining strategies for developing housing that would be affordable for families earning 50 to 80 percent of the statewide median income. MEDA engaged SWMHP to help develop an action plan.

Planning for the project began in 2000, when MEDA and SWMHP began evaluating potential sites. They settled on a 40-acre site located just northwest of Marshall's downtown. The land was purchased with funds derived from a tax increment financing (TIF) bond issue. The construction plan was to build in two phases, with sales from the first phase helping to fund the second. SWMHP was expecting a six-year time frame to build out both phases, but the whole site was built and occupied in only three years. Phase I, which consisted of 42 single-family lots and 18 rental townhomes, was sold out by January 2003.

Financing and Programs

The Southwest Minnesota Housing Partnership was founded in 1992 by four community-based organizations concerned with population loss and the stabilization of the region's economic base in order to stay vital. SWMHP serves its original 14-county service area. It has developed, rehabilitated, or financed 4,079 units to date, bringing an investment of over $150 million to the region. SWMHP has formed a staff of 11 professionals with experience in planning, construction, finance, and asset management. The partnership continually works to expand and improve its services and now offers planning, construction management, program administration, project fiscal management, lending, grant writing, marketing, education, and mortgage counseling.

In order to make Marshall Parkway affordable for lower-income residents, SWMHP had to employ a number of different affordable financing strategies. These strategies can be divided into four different types: reduction of land costs, reduction of construction costs, first mortgage products, and special mortgage products. Land acquisition costs were reduced using tax increment financing. TIF funds were used to purchase the land and make

infrastructure improvements. The cost for individual lots was only $3,200. Construction costs were reduced through a Schwan's construction loan. Schwan's Food Company built four homes using out-of-pocket funds.

Planning and Design

The site plan for the project, now called Marshall Parkway, called for 78 single-family units, three duplex lots, and two multifamily buildings, one with 18 units and the other with 30. Homes and duplexes are built in a variety of styles that include ranch, neocolonial, and split-level. Some homes have front porches. The site plan was designed to integrate into the surrounding neighborhood, with the goal of stimulating more adjacent residential development. The streets were laid out in a grid pattern that created six blocks. One long block on the east side of Marshall Parkway would transition into the

Concerned about employee recruitment and retention, Schwan's Food Company financially assisted the development of affordable homes at Marshall Parkway.

All single-family detached homes—the affordable as well as the market-rate ones—have a two-car garage.

The market-rate single-family homes in the community are slightly larger, and have more expensive finishes and more exterior detail.

existing neighborhood. The multifamily dwellings would occupy the north side of the development. The remaining land would be divided into five blocks designed around a park that would also function as a stormwater retention area. These blocks each contain between six and 16 single-family and duplex units.

The site plan works largely within Marshall's existing zoning, which is a standard suburban-style code. Lot sizes in the development are 60 feet wide by 125 feet deep with 25-foot setbacks. Each home has a two-car garage, and all multifamily units have designated off-street parking. Streetscape enhancements include sidewalks and trees planted throughout the development. The affordable units in the development differ slightly from the market-rate units in two ways: they have slightly smaller square footage, and they have less expensive finishing and exterior details.

Affordability and Management/Marketing

MEDA's investment in the project leveraged additional local money including funds from the Greater Minnesota Housing Fund (GMHF), the Minnesota Housing Finance Agency, and Schwan's Food Company. These funds went toward constructing homes and providing downpayment and other financial assistance to homebuyers. All but ten of the single-family units constructed at Marshall Parkway are considered affordable. The affordability of these units is largely guaranteed by a number of financing products available to potential homebuyers. These products come from a variety of agencies including federal, state, and nonprofit organizations. SWMHP's role is to steer potential homebuyers to the financing product that best fits their needs. The variety of financing products has helped guarantee a mix of incomes at

Marshall Parkway. In general, purchasers must earn less than 80 percent of the statewide median income.

SWMHP maximizes the affordability of homes through the aggressive use of first mortgage products. SWMHP used three different first mortgage programs at Marshall Parkway: the Community Activity Set Aside program (CASA), the HUD Rural Redevelopment 502 Direct Participation Loan Program, and the Guaranteed Loan Program. Regardless of which program is used, the process starts with homebuyer education and mortgage counseling for qualified buyers.

CASA, a program run by the Minnesota Housing Finance Agency, is funded through the sale of tax-exempt single-family mortgage revenue bonds. The program is an income-restricted product for first-time homebuyers that range from one-half to one point below conventional financing.

Funded by the U.S. Department of Housing and Urban Development (HUD), the Rural Redevelopment 502 Direct Loan Program is a low-interest product designed to help low-income rural residents acquire housing. The product has interest rates pegged to income, with the lowest rate being 1 percent, over a 33-year loan term.

SWMHP offered two special mortgage products to potential Marshall Parkway homebuyers: an affordable gap loan and an entry cost assistance loan. If they wish to access the gap and entry cost assistance loans, all potential borrowers are required to take homebuyer education classes, work with mortgage and budget counselors, and use 28 percent of their gross income for housing costs. Housing costs are defined as the amount of income that can be used to make principal, interest, insurance, and tax escrow payments. Since the gap loan

Two multifamily buildings were constructed, including 48 units of affordable and market-rate rental units.

is based on the "gap" between the maximum loan a buyer can access and the cost of the house, the amount of the loan has varied from several hundred dollars to maximum amount allowed of $25,000. The GMHF also offers a 0 percent gap loan, which is due when the mortgage is paid off or refinanced, or the home is sold.

The entry cost assistance loan is a 0 percent deferred loan offered by the SWMHP. It comes due when the first mortgage is paid off or refinanced, the home is sold, or it ceases to be owner occupied. The loan amount is determined by closing costs excluding "prepaid" amounts. Prepaids are the first year's real estate taxes and insurance premium that is required by the lender at closing. The entry cost assistance loan provides two-thirds of the needed closing costs. Closing costs for homes at Marshall Parkway have averaged $2,700 per home, with the entry cost assistance loan paying an average of $1,800 per home. The borrower must supply $900 (one-third), plus the required prepayments on taxes and insurance.

The success of Marshall Parkway has prompted SWMHP, the city, and Schwan's to embark on the development of Marshall Parkway II. All the stakeholders wanted to improve the master plan and individual building architecture in Marshall Parkway II. They have partnered with the Building Better Neighborhoods Program to achieve this goal. The mission of the Building Better Neighborhoods Program is to foster the creation of safe, decent, and affordable housing within cohesive, well-planned, and economically balanced neighborhoods. The program helps communities like Marshall that are new to developing affordable housing to address issues of preserving community character and appeal through good planning, site design, and building design.

In a small town, word of mouth is the best marketing strategy. Several sources provided the initial spark to generate local discussion about Marshall Parkway. Schwan's helped pique interest by sending out information about the project in employees' paychecks. By holding an open house, SWMHP gave the community a chance to see the product available in Marshall Parkway. The Marshall Independent newspaper was vocal in its support of Marshall Parkway throughout its development.

Lessons Learned

■ Employer-assisted housing is feasible in smaller towns. In fact, it is probably a better fit in smaller towns, where the relationship among firms, local government, and the community is stronger than in larger metropolitan areas, where those connections are less tractable. There also is a potentially greater need for companies to play a role in providing affordable housing in smaller markets because fewer inexpensive housing options generally are available there.

■ TIF bonds, used to purchase the 40 acres upon which Marshall Parkway was built, helped reduce the cost of land acquisition, which was passed on to homebuyers.

■ Shortly after Marshall officials decided to address affordable housing in the community, they realized that they did not have the institutional capacity to develop a successful housing strategy on their own. By partnering with SWMHP, they aligned themselves with an organization that could provide the technical expertise the community needed to succeed.

■ The involvement of a major employer was critical to the process. For years, Schwan's had been giving back to the Marshall community through a number of projects and programs. This resulted in a strong foundation for cooperation between the city and Schwan's. Working together to build affordable housing for the community's workforce was an important goal for both parties. Besides contributing financial support for the project, Schwan's involvement added credibility and helped legitimize the concept of affordable housing development within the community.

■ SWMHP's experience in Marshall and throughout rural southwest Minnesota has convinced the partnership that homebuyer education is very important. Many people in rural areas feel they could never afford to buy their own home. Showing people the path to homeownership not only improves lives, but also can be a powerful marketing tool.

University Glen at California State University–Channel Islands: Camarillo, California

Through an innovative development and financing strategy, California State University and UniDev LLC have created affordable for-sale housing for faculty and staff by using surplus land to construct single-family residences, townhomes, apartments, and retail space. The market-rate apartments, retail, and other programs assist with making the development self-funding.

UNIVERSITY GLEN FACTS

Land Use: A total of 414 housing units will be constructed on site. Ninety-eight will be affordable for-sale houses–36 single-family homes and 62 townhouses. There will be 316 market-rate rental units (namely, 60 rental townhouses and 256 apartments), 58 of which will be constructed over the commercial space.

Affordability: University Glen provides affordable for-sale housing to faculty and staff of California State University's Channel Islands campus as well as market-rate rental housing. Priority is given to faculty and staff for the purchase of the for-sale housing. Houses are sold for roughly 65 percent of market value. Annual home price appreciation is capped at the Consumer Price Index (CPI) and the land is leased from the California State University–Channel Islands Site Authority.

FUNDING/PROGRAMS

Funding: Tax-exempt bonds, Citibank FSB construction loans, Fannie Mae low-interest loans.

Programs: Mello-Roos Community Facility District, land leases, home price appreciation caps.

Developer: UniDev LLC, Bethesda, Maryland.

Architects: Lim Chang Rohling & Associates (Pasadena, California); McLarand Vasquez Emsiek & Partners, Inc. (Irvine, California); WFA Architecture and Planning, Inc. (Laguna Beach, California); William Hezmalhalch Architects, Inc. (Santa Ana, California); the Withee Malcolm Partnership, Architects (Torrance, California).

General Description

Skyrocketing housing values in California have made recruitment and retention of faculty and staff difficult at many state universities. With the median price of a home in the state fast approaching $500,000, less than 20 percent of households there can afford a median priced home. California State University–Channel Islands in Camarillo, California, is the 23rd campus of California State University and will eventually serve 15,000 full-time students. Being the newest campus in the state university system meant extensive recruiting for the entire academic staff. Despite the natural beauty of the area and the competitive salaries offered, university planners found that even the higher-paid university professors were deterred by California's expensive housing market. Realizing it had a recruitment and retention problem, the university responded with an innovative method of providing affordable for-sale housing for faculty and staff and market-rate rental apartments.

Located in Camarillo in Ventura County, the university is roughly 50 miles northwest of Los Angeles, 40 miles southeast of Santa Barbara, and about 15 minutes from the Pacific Ocean. The university is located on the site of the former Camarillo State Mental Hospital, which opened in 1936 and closed in 1997. At its peak, the hospital housed close to 15,000 patients and staff. Due to its proximity to Los Angeles, it had several high-profile patients including jazz great Charlie Parker, who wrote "Relaxin' at Camarillo" about his time at the hospital. The university has renovated and converted some of the historic buildings for campus use. New campus structures and parking are being constructed with an eye toward compatibility with the style of the historic hospital. Long-range plans call for complete campus buildout in 2030.

The California State University–Channel Islands Site Authority was created in 1998 with the specific mission of transitioning the hospital to use as a university with additional compatible uses. A seven-person board comprising four representatives from the trustees of California State University and three members from Ventura County governs the site authority. They are responsible for managing the purchase and sale of government bonds to fund construction of the university, overseeing the aesthetic integrity of University Glen, and establishing policies that control residents' use of the area. A nonprofit corporation, the University Glen Corporation, was established to handle the day-to-day operations of the residential community and to ensure the continuing affordability of the units.

Development Process

The university property features 204 acres divided into two sectors: the West Campus and the East Campus. The West Campus comprises 42 developed acres, including the old hospital site, and is being developed for academic uses. The East Campus contains 162 acres of developable land on which the housing and commercial development are being built. Construction on the East Campus began in October 2000 and is scheduled for completion in 2006.

The site authority initially turned to San Francisco–based Catellus Development Corporation for development of the housing component. The firm proposed developing all market-rate housing on the site with a financial return to the university. Market-rate housing in California, however, was not likely to be affordable to the faculty and staff of the university. The authority then turned to Bethesda, Maryland–based UniDev LLC, a company with extensive experience with development of both university and af-

fordable housing. In 2000, they were brought on as the owner's representative to manage the planning, design, financing, and implementation of the redevelopment of the East Campus.

UniDev proposed having the site authority lease the land to the homeowners, ensuring a continuing income stream. In addition, incorporating market-rate apartments open to the public would provide an income stream to fund campus construction and renovation as

(Above) California State University at Channel Islands is nestled in rolling hills with no direct neighbors and no community opposition to the proposed development of the new community.

(Left) The market-rate rental apartments at University Glen create an ongoing income stream that helps subsidize the affordable housing units.

well as the continuation of the affordable homeownership program. In all, a total of 414 residences were proposed. A total of 256 apartments were to be constructed, with 58 to be built over 30,000 square feet of retail space. A total of 98 for-sale homes were proposed: 36 single-family homes and 62 townhouses. In addition, 60 rental townhomes were proposed.

UniDev worked extensively with faculty and staff and the site authority to craft a plan that would serve everyone's needs. The faculty and staff of the university needed affordable housing. The site authority needed a dedicated and consistent revenue stream to fund campus expansion and renovation needs, as well as maintain the affordability of the on-campus housing. UniDev proposed developing the site in phases to stagger the move-in dates and create cash flow to fund the affordable units.

University Workforce Housing

Faced with recruitment and retention problems, partly based on the inability of faculty and staff to find acceptable affordable housing, many universities are seeking creative ways to provide affordable housing to their faculty and staff.

California Universities

While the problem of housing costs affecting the recruitment and retention of university staff and faculty is a nationwide problem, it is most severe on both coasts, with California being the most severely affected state. Several in the University of California (UC) and California State University (CSU) system have been addressing this problem for years. UC–Irvine was probably a pioneer with the concept of providing faculty housing on land that is leased to faculty on a 99-year lease. This lowers costs for faculty homeowners while generating cash flow to finance continuing affordable housing efforts. Other California universities using or planning to use this technique are UC–Santa Barbara, CSU–Fullerton, and CSU–Monterey Bay. Most accompany the lease with home price appreciation caps. A variety of other programs including low-interest loans, shared appreciation mortgages, housing allowances, and down-payment assistance are offered at many California universities, including Stanford, helping faculty and staff find acceptable affordable housing.

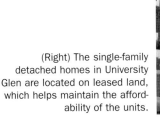

(Above) The architectural style of the community is Spanish colonial and Monterrey, reflecting the style of the renovated historic structures on campus. Shown here are rental townhomes.

(Right) The single-family detached homes in University Glen are located on leased land, which helps maintain the affordability of the units.

The development site is nestled in a valley between rolling hills with no adjacent neighbors except for the university. Because of the relative isolation of the site, there was no significant community opposition to this project. Some stream restoration and wetland mitigation were required and groundhog tunneling was a recurring problem. Because of the financing sources for the project, "prevailing wage" requirements were applicable to all construction.

Financing and Programs

Tax-exempt bonds and a 100 percent loan-to-value loan from Fannie Mae and Citibank were used to finance the project. In addition, the Mello-Roos Community Facilities District Act was used to fund site improvements. Spearheaded by California state senator Henry Mello and assemblyman Mike Roos, the legislation was passed by the California legislature in 1982. The act passed in response to Proposition 13, which limited the ability of local governments and developers to finance new projects.

Mello-Roos permits any county, city, special district, or school district or joint powers authority to establish a Mello-Roos Community Facilities District (CFD). This allows for financing of streets, sewer systems, and other basic infrastructure along with providing police and fire protection, ambulance service, schools, parks, libraries, etc. A two-thirds majority of the residents located within the boundaries of the proposed district must agree to the establishment of the district. Once established, a special tax lien is placed against all property in the district. If bonds were issued by the CFD, the taxes are assessed annually until the bond is paid off.

Planning and Design

The Spanish colonial and Monterey architectural style of the renovated historic buildings of the Camarillo State Mental Hospital that were converted to campus uses set the design theme for the new residential construction at University Glen. Stucco walls and red tile roofing enclose modern conveniences, including category 5 wiring for high-bandwidth applications in all bedrooms and family and living areas. The site for the homes is quite spectacular. Located adjacent to the uni-

versity in a secluded area surrounded by rolling hills and colorful orchards, the relatively dense development has pedestrian access to the university while maintaining its peaceful residential character. Since most residents will be able to walk to it, the construction of 30,000 square feet of retail space will add to the pedestrian-friendly nature of the housing on site.

The market-rate rental apartments range in size from 680 square feet for a one-bedroom, one-bathroom apartment to almost 1,800 square feet for the three-bedroom with a den, 2.5 bathrooms, a fireplace, and a two-car garage.

The townhouses are available in several configurations and two basic styles: the Arroyo and the Monterey. The Arroyo townhouse comes in three floor plans ranging from 1,300 to 1,600 square feet. The two-story, two-bedroom, 2.5-bathroom townhouses are constructed in groups of two to four units per building. At 1,460 to 1,800 square feet, the Monterey townhouses are larger and available in three different floor plans as well. They are two stories tall, but have three bedrooms with 2.5 bathrooms and are constructed in groups of two to six units per building.

The single-family homes are available in four floor plans ranging from 1,700 to 2,300 square feet. The two-story residences will all have three bedrooms with a choice of 2.5 or 3.5 bathrooms. All units have an attached two-car garage.

Affordability and Management/Marketing

Though offered to the general public, the market-rate apartments are popular with CSU staff because of their proximity to the school. The apartments have been mostly fully leased since opening. At the time of publication, rents ranged from $1,200 to $2,200 per month, about 10 percent below current market rate.

Although the for-sale housing is offered to the general public as well, priority is given to faculty and staff of the university. Demand is such that all units were sold to CSU faculty and staff. Keeping the units technically available to the general public keeps the sales in good stead with the Fair Housing Act of 1968 while providing much-needed shelter for faculty and staff who otherwise would be unable to afford for-sale residences in the expensive Camarillo housing market. There is currently a waiting list to purchase the for-sale units in the development.

For-sale townhouses and single-family homes are sold at roughly 65 percent of market value to qualified buyers. The first phase of for-sale residences sold out quickly. Sale prices for the single-family homes ranged from $225,000 to $307,000. Townhouse prices started at $166,000. Since the land is leased, the homeowner owns only the house and its appreciation is capped at annual increases equal to the Consumer Price Index (CPI). Values can be adjusted for home improvements made to the house. A nonprofit corporation has been created to function as a homeowners association with the additional responsibility of addressing future affordability issues. Upon sale of the house, the seller pays 1 percent of the sale price into a fund controlled by the nonprofit that ensures future affordability of the units. The buyer pays an additional 5 percent into this fund. The nonprofit also can establish new home values upon resale of the unit. Units are required to remain affordable, but there is discretion regarding reestablishing new sales cost.

Land lease payments and rent from the market-rate apartments are expected to generate $800 million to the site authority over a 45-year period. The revenue generated will go toward bond repayment ($300 million) and will fund university programs and additional campus construction and renovation.

Lessons Learned

■ Including market-rate rental units can generate the cash flow needed to support the development of affordable for-sale housing for faculty and staff.

■ Leasing the land rather than selling it with the for-sale housing also creates additional cash flow that can ensure that the for-sale units remain affordable.

■ Capping the appreciation of the for-sale units allows owners to make money on their investment while maintaining future affordability because home price appreciation in most markets far exceeds the CPI.

■ Providing a mix of housing product types permits the developer to respond to a broad variety of households with a wide range of incomes.

■ A large phasing plan can create stress and complications with a large number of people moving in at the same time.

■ Know the parking requirements of your market. Most markets in California are particularly auto dependent, with most households having at least two cars. Additional parking was added to the original plan as the required 1.7 parking ratio turned out to be inadequate.

Murphy Park: St. Louis, Missouri

Through lowering the density, creating significant new infrastructure, and forming innovative partnerships, developer McCormack Baron Salazar, Inc., has transformed a blighted high-rise public housing project into a safe and thriving mixed-income community. Of particular interest is the developer's partnership with the local school board and private sector interests to improve the local elementary school.

General Description

The area north of downtown St. Louis has experienced disinvestment owing to decades of out-migration, industrial decline, and slum clearance programs. During the 1950s and 1960s, several high-rise public housing projects were built over what was once a working-class neighborhood. After 30 years of neglect and disrepair, one of those projects was razed in a demonstration program by the U.S. Department of Housing and Urban Development, ushering in a new era of mixed-income housing projects. The George L. Vaughn Family Apartments gave way to Murphy Park, a 413-unit development of two-, three-, and four-bedroom rental townhouses and apartments.

Murphy Park was built by St. Louis–based developer McCormack Baron Salazar (MBS). MBS is a for-profit firm specializing in the development of economically integrated urban neighborhoods. Since 1973, MBS has developed more than 11,500 units of affordable and market-rate housing in 100 developments in 24 cities across the United States. The firm strives to revitalize entire neighborhoods by creating a catalyst for reinvestment through its developments.

Development Process

The George L. Vaughn Family Apartments consisted of four nondescript high rises built in the style typical of public housing projects constructed during the 1950s. Located just north of downtown and within blocks of the infamous Pruitt-Igoe projects, the 656 units in the towers had fallen into severe disrepair by the early 1990s and were virtually vacant. Existing governmental housing programs required that one affordable unit be built for every unit torn down. This well-intentioned requirement proved prohibitive when it came to replacing very high-density urban public housing such as Vaughn. The Cranston-Gonzalez National Affordable Housing Act of 1992 eased the replacement ratio to one new unit for every two units removed. HUD foreclosed on the property, and agreed to sell it to the St. Louis Housing Authority. The Housing Authority demolished three of the four old towers and leased the land to McCormack Baron for $1 a year. Additional adjacent land for later phases was voluntarily sold to the city or taken by eminent domain.

The city of St. Louis initially wanted all low-income housing to replace Vaughn. A special task force convened by then-Mayor Freeman Bosley determined that the north side of St. Louis was overwhelmed with public housing. The committee's recommendation was to build some market-rate housing to attract wealthier people and investment into the area. A compromise was reached whereby Murphy Park would be developed as a mixed-income community.

Murphy Park was developed in three phases, the first opening in 1996 and the last in 2003. All 413 units are rentals. Apartments are available in townhouse or garden-style configurations with two-, three-, and four-bedroom floor plans. Lease-up was very quick, and today Murphy Park maintains 98 percent occupancy.

Financing and Programs

Federal funds for demolishing the Vaughn public housing complex and creating a demonstration housing program were earmarked in the Cranston-Gonzalez National Affordable Housing Act. The St. Louis Housing Authority administered these funds. The "demonstration" part of the project involved using public dollars to leverage private investment in the project. This "mixed finance" approach to affordable housing funding would later serve as the prototype for the HOPE VI program.

The total construction cost of Murphy Park was $60 million, spread across three phases of development. Public housing development and capital funds made up the largest block of funding at $28.4 million. The city of St. Louis spent a total of $4.7 million to upgrade public infrastructure such as parks, drainage, and utilities connections. The Missouri Housing Development Commission supplied the project's first mortgage of $7.2 million. These public sector investments helped the project leverage private funding to pay for the rest of construction costs. Private tax credit equity raised $15.4 million. Corporate donations to the project totaled $4 million, including $3.5 million donated by COVAM, a not-for-profit community development corporation made up of stakeholders with interests in the vicinity of Murphy Park.

(Top) The townhouse units of Murphy Park have the exterior appearance of a single-family home, although each building contains two to four units.

(Bottom) All of the streets in Murphy Park have sidewalks enhancing the development's pedestrian friendliness and community atmosphere.

Just north of downtown St. Louis, Murphy Park was constructed on the site of the former George L. Vaughn Family Apartments public housing project. The four high-rise towers that made up the Vaughn apartments were demolished in the 1990s and replaced by the lower-density development.

Planning and Design

For the project's architects and developers, it was important to design Murphy Park to be very different than the Vaughn towers. Murphy Park's total density is 37 percent lower than that of the Vaughn towers. Parking is placed behind buildings and on the street. All streets running through the development have sidewalks, enhancing the area's pedestrian friendliness and community atmosphere.

Each building is designed to be slightly different than the next. Bay windows, brickwork, porches, columns, and turret-style sitting rooms are found in varying configurations. The architectural variety helps reinforce the notion that Murphy Park is not simply a public housing development, but is instead a mixed-income community. Buildings are designed in a "mansion" style, resembling one large home. However, each structure contains two to four units, each with its own exterior entrance. Landscaping and green space help disguise the density of the project.

Affordability and Management/Marketing

Murphy Park is managed by McCormack Baron Ragan, a subsidiary company of the project's developer. The firm also manages three market-rate, six mixed-income, and eight income-restricted/Section 8 properties scattered throughout the St. Louis metropolitan area. All applicants for housing are screened for criminal back-

grounds and given credit checks. Besides handling its management duties, McCormack Baron Ragan connects residents with social services provided by local charities and government. Child care is provided on site, and management promotes youth after-school programs, job training, and health services.

Marketing of Murphy Park is done mostly by word of mouth. Public service announcements and occasional newspaper advertisements make people aware of apartment openings. Many families are referred to Murphy Park by city agencies.

Murphy Park has attracted a wide range of family incomes. Families from all income groups want their children to attend the best schools. Since Jefferson Elementary is one of the best schools in St. Louis, families find the idea of living in Murphy Park very attractive. In 2004, 110 families with an annual household income greater than $30,000 leased market-rate apartments, including 15 who make more than $60,000. Upper-middle-income people live alongside households on public assistance in apartments that cannot be distinguished from each other. Market-rate renters are also eager to live at Murphy Park because of its proximity to downtown. Renters who qualify for tax credit or public housing also reap the same benefits. Murphy Park represents a step up in the quality, size, and appearance of housing for affordable housing residents.

Jefferson Elementary School

St. Louis, Missouri

Early in the development process, it became clear to McCormack Baron Salazar CEO Richard Baron that resurrecting the distressed area north of downtown St. Louis meant more than simply constructing new housing. Schools in the area were in very poor condition, with no air conditioning or functioning computers. Prior to 1998, few neighborhood children attended the local Jefferson Elementary School. Due to court-ordered public school desegregation, the approximately 750 school-aged children in the area were bussed to 60 different schools in St. Louis County.

Richard Baron approached the St. Louis Board of Education about converting the Jefferson Elementary School into a neighborhood school that would serve children in the surrounding community. The principal of the school was replaced so that a new, more innovative curriculum could be implemented. Baron agreed to raise the funds needed to upgrade the school and train new teachers.

The private sector agreed to play a significant role in the redevelopment of Jefferson School. Southwestern Bell made a $762,500 commitment to the school, including wiring the entire building for Internet access and underwriting the cost of the University of Missouri's Center for Technology Innovations in Education to assist with the integration of technology into the curriculum. The Danforth Foundation contributed $300,000 toward the professional development of new faculty, allowing teachers to develop their full potential as educators and integrate technology into their classes. In total, corporate and nonprofit contributions totaled over $4 million to upgrade, equip, and staff the school.

The surrounding community and St. Louis as a whole have lauded the new and improved Jefferson Elementary School. It is now considered one of the best schools—if not *the* best school—in the St. Louis County School District. With its new neighborhood school status, 272 students of the enrollment (68 percent of total) came from the surrounding area in 2000. Parents who had enrolled their students in magnet schools withdrew their children so they could attend Jefferson. The school has proven to be a powerful tool to attract higher-income families to Murphy Park and other adjacent housing developments. These higher-income families tend to rent the market-rate units at Murphy Park or buy one of the for-sale homes that have recently been constructed nearby by other developers.

Given the success that Jefferson Elementary has had in the community, the St. Louis Public School District has made a commitment to enhancing the middle and high schools that serve the area. The brand-new Vashon High School, located about a mile from Murphy Park, was recently completed at a cost of $40 million. Upgrades are currently underway on Gateway Middle School. In time, students living in Murphy Park will be able to attend all three of these high-quality neighborhood schools. McCormack Baron Salazar's involvement in the community not only has given many students a pleasant and safe place to live, but it also has brought them a high-quality education.

Murphy Park has a three-tiered rent structure: market rate, tax credit, and public housing. Rents range from $150 a month for a two-bedroom public housing unit to $775 a month for a four-bedroom townhouse. The difference between market-rate rent and tax credit rent is relatively small—only about $80 a month. This is a reflection of the weak apartment rental market in St. Louis. In other cities served by McCormack Baron Ragan, market-rate rents are often double the tax credit rate.

The ratio of market-rate, tax-credit income-restricted, and public housing units remains the same, although individual apartments are not earmarked as any one type. Thirty-two percent of the complex (132 units) is rented to households paying market-rate rent. Households making less than 80 percent of the area median income of $60,400 are eligible for public housing units. In practice, residents living in public housing units are making 15 to 20 percent of the area median income, since government resources are directed toward the people most in need. Units reserved for households on public assistance make up 54 percent of Murphy Park (223 units). The remaining 14 percent (56 units) are reserved for households making less than 60 percent of area median income by virtue of tax credit restrictions. Affordability restrictions are not tied to individual units. Only the ratio of market-rate/tax-credit/public units is maintained. If a household on public assistance experiences a rise in income, they can stay in the same unit and begin paying market-rate rent.

Lessons Learned

■ For families, the desirability of an area often lies in the quality of schools there. Long a contributory factor in the suburbanization of America, urban schools should be improved by any means necessary to attract people back to the city center. Good schools help attract middle- and upper-income people to a mixed-income community.

■ In weak-market cities or depressed areas, a low or zero land cost can be a major advantage. Even though market-rate and affordable rents will be low, the absence of land acquisition cost greatly reduces the upfront cost to the developer.

■ Affordability within a mixed-income development does not have to be tied to a particular unit. By "floating" the affordable designation, families whose income rises above affordability levels can stay in their unit and begin paying market-rate rent.

■ Developers and management companies can connect social services and job education to their tenants.

First Ward Place: Charlotte, North Carolina

First Ward Place is a thriving mixed-income community that replaces a failed public housing project in Charlotte. The new community provides affordable and market-rate housing. Lower-income households are offered housing options and educational services designed to help lift them out of poverty and eventually to homeownership.

FIRST WARD PLACE FACTS

Land Use: Five hundred thirty-three total units of mixed-income, mixed-density housing on 27 acres. Local amenities such as a child care center and a community services center are also on site.

Affordability: Two hundred fifty-five units of public housing, where beneficiaries rent property but are expected to make the transition to ownership or market rentals within a specified time period. Another 50 units are price controlled and reserved for those making 80 percent of the area median income due to Low Income Housing Tax Credits. Finally, 101 ownership and rental units are available for occupancy at market rates.

FUNDING/PROGRAMS

Funding: HOPE VI grants, Low Income Housing Tax Credits.

Programs: Community Redevelopment/Housing Agency, money management and homebuyer education.

Developer: NationsBank Community Development Corporation (Charlotte, North Carolina).

Architect: FMK Architects (Charlotte, North Carolina).

General Description

The Charlotte Housing Authority (CHA) and Nations-Bank (now Bank of America) Community Development Corporation joined with the Charlotte-Mecklenburg Planning Commission to create a comprehensively planned, new community that has breathed new life into Charlotte's First Ward neighborhood. The result was First Ward Place, a 406-unit, mixed-income, mixed-density community located on 27 acres adjacent to the central business district in downtown Charlotte, North Carolina. The project includes the complete redevelopment of Earle Village, a failed 409-unit public housing project built in 1966 under the auspices of urban renewal. Today, Charlotte's First Ward is an economically and racially diverse neighborhood incorporating 283 units of low- to moderate-income rental housing, 68 units for seniors at Autumn Place, and 55 market-rate, low-income, and affordable homeownership units. Integrated into the community is a comprehensive supportive services program that assists residents in attaining the goal of self-sufficiency, including the skills necessary for homeownership, one of this country's greatest wealth-building engines.

Forty-seven percent of the rental units and one-third of the for-sale townhouses are reserved for public housing–eligible households. All of these households are required to participate in the CHA's Family Self-Sufficiency (FSS) Program. The FSS Program is designed to help individuals and families become financially independent and to make the transition out of public housing within the mandatory five-year limit. The program provides educational and job opportunities as well as vocational training, caseworkers to oversee participants' medical needs, childcare, and money-management training. This program, developed by CHA, has become a national model for helping public housing residents become independent of government assistance. An integral part of CHA's FSS Program is the

Home Ownership Institute, which teaches participants the responsibilities of homeownership, credit repair, and budgeting. At the end of the 13-month course, graduates may purchase one of the subsidized for-sale houses in First Ward Place. Graduates of the FSS Program who do not qualify for one of the subsidized for-sale houses may elect to live in one of the market-rate rentals.

Development Process

In 1966, the 409-unit Earle Village housing project was completed on the site. A model of poorly designed public housing, Earle Village quickly devolved into a center of crime, poverty, and decay. By the early 1990s, occupancy had dropped to about 60 percent, and the city made its restoration and rehabilitation a priority. The Charlotte Housing Authority (CHA) rejected plans to rehabilitate Earle Village, and chose to pursue a HOPE VI grant to create a more sustainable, mixed-income option for the First Ward. CHA received its first HOPE VI grant in 1993, and it was supplemented in 1995 to provide a total of $41.7 million.

(Top) The quality of the mixed-income community is such that the market-rate units are very popular.

(Right) New urbanist principles were employed in the planning and design of First Ward Place, creating a strong sense of place and community.

Construction began in 1994. The project was developed in five phases over a period of three years. All of the rental housing was built in the first two phases. The community center and units for seniors were built during the third phase. Single-family homes and townhouses were built in the fourth and fifth phases, respectively.

First Ward Place includes 283 one-, two-, three-, and four-bedroom rental apartments and two-, three-, four-, and five-bedroom townhouses. Eighteen percent of the rental units are designated for residents earning less than 55 percent of the area median income and were financed using low-income housing tax credit equity. Thirty-five percent of the rental units house residents pay market-rate rents. The remaining rental units are leased to public housing–eligible households through the CHA. Monthly rent and utilities are limited to 30 percent of household annual income. As household income rises, rents increase proportionally. As is the case with most HOPE VI projects, the subsidized units are indistinguishable from the market-rate units.

First Ward Place comprises other types of housing. The HOPE VI revitalization of the First Ward also includes Autumn Place, which houses seniors who relocated from other public housing properties. Autumn Place has 66

one- and two-bedroom apartments and was 100 percent funded through the HOPE VI grant. In addition, 55 for-sale townhouses and single-family homes are available to people of all ages. More than a third of these for-sale homes were reserved for former CHA residents who graduated from the CHA's Home Ownership Institute. The remaining units were sold to market-rate buyers at prices up to $160,000. The funding for the single-family homes was 85 percent private and 15 percent HOPE VI.

Financing and Programs

CHA initially engaged NationsBank Community Development Corporation to serve as a development consultant. Later, the bank agreed to act as a development partner and to create a mixed-finance development under the HOPE VI program. NationsBank secured approximately $10 million in low-income housing tax credit equity needed to subsidize the low-income units. NationsBank did not collect a development fee but receives half of any income the project generates after expenses. The $41.7 million HOPE VI grant contributed to funding part of the development costs of the project, demolition, design, construction, and administrative costs. CHA continues to own the land, and the improved buildings are owned by First Ward Place LLC, in which NationsBank and CHA are board members.

Planning and Design

The First Ward Plan was sponsored by a public/private initiative to plan for the entire First Ward while Earle Village was being rebuilt. There were a number of issues to contend with, including large vacant tracts of land, a nearby prison and court facilities, two congested highways, and a widespread perception of the First Ward as the most dangerous area of the city.

The plan incorporates a series of infrastructure changes to help create a residentially driven reinvestment program. Local streets were reconfigured to create a grid-pattern road network. The major traffic artery into downtown—Seventh Street—was spruced up and turned into a landscaped boulevard. A new linear park was built and connected to a greenway system to the south.

The plan divides the First Ward into distinct precincts, each with its own character. However, the urban character between neighborhoods remains unbroken by fences or large arterial roads. Buildings were designed to mimic the surrounding early 20th-century areas of Charlotte. A recreation center and three blocks of housing were built along Seventh Street, the spine of the First Ward. This showed potential residents that serious redevelopment was occurring, and the project gained substantial momentum.

First Ward Place replaced the crime-ridden Earle Village public housing project. The new community is economically and racially diverse and includes a strong system of support services designed to allow residents to improve their economic situation.

Affordability and Management/Marketing

First Ward Place was one of the first HOPE VI projects funded by the U.S. Department of Housing and Urban Development. Several procedures that would become standard for HOPE VI projects evolved as this and other early HOPE VI projects progressed. Founded in 1992, the HOPE VI program was intended to replace the failing housing programs of earlier decades. Instead of concentrating public housing into dense, self-contained settings, HOPE VI seeks to place it in a mixed-density and mixed-income setting. When public housing is mixed with other housing price points, many urban problems such as crime, disrepair, and lack of jobs are mitigated. Currently, older public housing structures are being torn down, reducing the number of affordable housing units. HOPE VI funds allow old affordable housing stock to be refurbished or rebuilt on the same site. A key innovation of the HOPE VI program is the incentive it created for public housing authorities to involve private developers in the creation of new mixed-income neighborhoods. HOPE VI and HUD's other mixed-finance development programs allow public housing funds to be combined with other public and private development funds to attract greater resources to projects. HUD estimates that the federal investment in HOPE VI will leverage a total of $7.49 billion in private funds.

Lessons Learned

■ The redevelopment of public housing is often a controversial issue, and both CHA and NationsBank were subjected to negative publicity from this project. The bank found itself in an unexpected and undesired position of having its investment in community redevelopment being criticized as a purely profit-driven means of gentrification. Both CHA and the bank worked hard to create better public relations and to assure the community that HOPE VI is not a wholesale displacement of low-income residents, but rather that the program contributes to community stabilization and enrichment.

■ A roughly equal number of dwelling units are found in First Ward Place before and after redevelopment. This displaces as few people as possible, and sustains surrounding retail uses.

■ The FSS Program, which is run by CHA, is critical for the ongoing success of this new mixed-income community. The property management company suggested that it would be helpful if HUD had established a set of guidelines outlining its expectations for property managers and social service providers.

■ The area surrounding a rehabilitated public housing development can also reap rewards. The neighborhood near First Ward Place has attracted significant amounts of outside investment since the project's completion.

New Pennley Place: Pittsburgh, Pennsylvania

Through an innovative partnership with the AFL-CIO labor union, assistance with land acquisition and assembly, and significant infrastructure improvements by the city of Pittsburgh, the Community Builders redeveloped this multiblock development by renovating one of the existing structures and building new ones.

NEW PENNLEY PLACE FACTS

Land Use: One hundred seventy-four rental apartments on 7.25 acres.

Affordability: Mixed-income rental housing typical of HOPE VI developments. 1) Sixty-six apartments and townhomes reserved for families earning 60 percent of the area median income (AMI) by virtue of Low Income Housing Tax Credit price restriction. 2) Thirty-eight additional units set aside for households earning 50 percent or less of the AMI due to Section 8 project-based subsidy. 3) Thirty-two "market-rate" rental apartments and duplexes priced to be affordable to families earning 80 percent of the AMI. 4) Thirty-eight apartments reserved for elderly (over 65) residents whose incomes do not exceed 50 percent of the AMI.

FUNDING/PROGRAMS

Funding: Low Income Housing Tax Credits, HOPE VI grants, Section 8 Project-Based Subsidy, and HUD Section 202 Elderly Housing Subsidy.

Programs: Labor union assistance, social services administration, and land dedication.

Developer: The Community Builders, Inc. (Pittsburgh, Pennsylvania).

Architect: Perkins Eastman Architects PC (New York, New York).

Contact:

Jennifer L. Chhatlani

Senior Media Specialist

Chicago Housing Authority

Office of Communications

626 West Jackson Boulevard, Second Floor

Chicago, Illinois 60661

312-742-9936

Fax: 312-258-1602

E-mail: JChhatla@thecha.org

General Description

The East Liberty neighborhood of Pittsburgh was once considered a fashionable area, and for the first half of the 20th century was regarded as a "second downtown." Urban renewal projects undertaken in the 1960s, however, disrupted the urban fabric of the neighborhood. The mid-1960s brought new highway construction and several mid- and high-rise apartments, which for a time were considered a fashionable place to live. One of those complexes, Pennley Park Apartments, was built on three consolidated city blocks. By the mid-1990s, Pennley Park had been sold to an absentee landlord who let the property fall into disrepair. Middle-class flight and economic decline had made Pennley Park Apartments a housing choice of last resort for many families. Few, if any, of those low-income families were living with the assistance of an affordable housing program.

Located about four miles from downtown Pittsburgh, the Pennley Park Apartments were targeted by the Community Builders for renovation. The Community Builders has developed more than 18,000 units of mixed-income and special-needs housing since 1964. Today, the firm manages 60 rental complexes nationwide housing over 16,000 residents.

Pennley Park Apartments was replaced with a mixed-income, mixed-age community called New Pennley Place. With 174 total dwelling units, New Pennley Place was able to accommodate most of the residents who wanted to stay. Through substantial rehabilitation of an aging building and the new construction of townhomes, tenants now have a better quality of life with less financial burden, in a neighborhood that is beginning to show signs of revitalization.

Developers often find it difficult to develop market-rent housing in cities with weak housing markets because of the relatively low rents and sales prices such markets command. However, as this project shows, the relative availability of affordable land (or free land in some cases) in weak-market cities can often assist in making mixed-income or affordable communities more financially feasible.

Development Process

The U.S. Department of Housing and Urban Development (HUD) served notice that it would foreclose on the Pennley Park Apartments in 1995. Several community-based groups joined with the Pittsburgh Redevelopment Authority to work with HUD and foster redevelopment of the site. Chosen as the developer, the Community Builders soon thereafter adopted a redevelopment plan. HUD foreclosed on the site and allocated a $4 million upfront grant for demolition and purchase of an adjacent nuisance bar. The property was soon conveyed to the Community Builders, and work began in 1998.

The American Federation of Labor–Congress of Industrial Organizations (AFL-CIO) helped finance the project, on the condition that union laborers were employed for construction. Labor unions were also better equipped to handle the removal of asbestos, which was prevalent throughout the site. All construction workers were union affiliated, including 66 who came from the surrounding area. Sixteen residents from the area gained admittance to the union through their work on New Pennley Place, virtually ensuring them gainful employment in the future. Nearly $1 million was returned to the community in the form of wages paid to local workers.

The Pennley Park Apartments in the East Liberty neighborhood of Pittsburgh, shown here prior to demolition of two of the structures, were once considered a desirable place to live. The apartments fell into disrepair in the 1990s, becoming a housing choice of last resort for many poor families.

As a former "superblock" site, city streets had been removed and several city blocks were consolidated into one parcel of land to accommodate the large-scale buildings to be constructed there. The city of Pittsburgh rebuilt Broad Street, a road that had been removed to consolidate the property in the 1960s. The $800,000 project helped restore the street grid system and connect the site to the surrounding neighborhood. More than $600,000 has been allocated to complete transportation engineering and pedestrian studies in the neighborhood. The city also invested $140,000 to build Garland Parklet, a "tot lot" directly adjacent to New Pennley Place.

New Pennley Place was built in three phases at a total cost of $23 million. The first phase consisted of 102 units, 64 of which were located in the substantially renovated remaining building of Pennley Park Apartments. Thirty-eight brand-new townhouses were built in freestanding, mansion-style structures. Thirty-four more townhomes were built during the second phase. The third and final phases consisted of a three-story, 38-unit apartment building reserved for seniors. Construction was completed in 2001.

Planning and Design

Since New Pennley Place is a small infill site, it needed to be well designed to capitalize on the available land. Of the three mid-rise apartment buildings on the property, two were razed. The remaining three-story structure underwent substantial renovation. The existing building consisted largely of efficiency and one-bedroom units. Renovating the interior required substantial work. Efficiencies were combined to create two-bedroom apartments, along with renovation of the existing one-bedroom units. Units on the lowest level were given exterior entranceways. Units on upper levels are accessed by elevators and interior hallways. A total of 64 units were completed in the renovated building, along with a community room and management office.

Running perpendicular to the renovated building is a long common landscaped area, bordered on both sides by townhouses with one-, two-, and three-bedroom floor plans. Townhomes were built in freestanding duplex and quadraplex structures, and each unit has a separate entrance and small porch area. Most townhomes can also be accessed from the rear, where parking is located. All townhomes and apartments have fully equipped modern kitchens and bathrooms.

At the far end of the common area lies a three-story, 38-unit building for seniors. Low-income seniors live in one-bedroom flats and have some communal facilities on the ground floor. Preconstruction focus groups with the area's elderly residents showed that seniors preferred to live in an area with a mix of ages, but preferred not to have young neighbors. The seniors' building gives elderly people a place to live that meets both criteria.

New Pennley Place is the first major residential investment project to take place in the East Liberty neighborhood in over 30 years. The development has already reinvigorated the struggling economy of the area. Home Depot arranged $11 million in public/private financing to build its first inner-city store in Pittsburgh. A Whole Foods market was recently completed, along with other neighborhood-serving retail. The Community Builders and other nonprofit developers own several properties in the area and are formulating plans that build on the success of New Pennley Place.

Affordability and Management/Marketing

New Pennley Place has several tiers of affordability requirements, a defining trait of HOPE VI projects. Thirty-two of the project's 174 units (or 18 percent) rent at a nominal market rate. These market-rate units are priced to be affordable to families earning 80 percent of the AMI of $54,000, although income screening is not required to rent. The table below shows the amount paid at market rate. Rents are adjusted from these figures based on the program in which a household participates, but in no case can it exceed 30 percent of their annual income.

New Pennley Place Rents

Type	Number of Units	Market-Rate Rent
Studio	11	$514
One-bedroom flat	59	$595–$625
Two-bedroom flat	34	$725–$750
Two-bedroom townhouse	24	$750
Three-bedroom townhouse	8	$850

Note: Units for seniors are not included.

New Pennley Place is a mixed-income, mixed-age community.

Price-restricted apartments account for 81 percent of the dwelling units at New Pennley Place. Rents vary according to household salary, and in no case exceed 30 percent of the household's income. Low Income Housing Tax Credits used to finance construction restrict 66 apartment and townhomes to families earning 60 percent of the AMI. Thirty-eight units financed by AFL-CIO–administered Section 8 project-based subsidy are rented to families earning 50 percent of the AMI. To live in the 38-unit seniors' building, tenants must earn less than 50 percent of

the AMI and be over 65 years of age. This is made possible due to assistance from HUD Section 202 subsidy.

When beginning the project, the Community Builders wanted to displace as few people as possible. Many residents of the former Pennley Park Apartments now rent at New Pennley Place. Most residents of Pennley Park were low income, yet few were receiving government assistance. The Community Builders helped them get qualified for government programs, and now those families live in new, high-quality apartments with far less oppressive housing costs. Finding new residents has not been an issue, as the waiting list for apartments has risen as high as 700.

New Pennley Place shares a resident services coordinator with other Community Builders properties nearby. The purpose of employing a resident services coordinator is to connect residents with applicable social services such as job training, health and wellness, and other life-skills programs. The impact on residents' lives has been substantial. The complex maintains 97 percent occupancy. Employment of working-age tenants is near 90 percent, and delinquent rent payments are few. The management is also pleased to report that there has been no documentation of illegal activity on the property—a substantial change from the crime-riddled days before redevelopment.

Lessons Learned

■ Mixed-income housing does not only mean having market-rate units existing side by side with affordable units. There are several types of affordable programs, and by combining them into one property, a diverse section of the population can avail themselves of assistance.

■ Working with local residents is a very important part of the process. From focus groups to relocation assistance to connecting residents with social services, the developer and property manager can have even more of a positive impact on people's lives.

Redeveloping the site at a lower density allowed for the creation of a landscaped common area that is bordered by the new townhouses.

Cabrini-Green Homes/Near North Redevelopment Initiative: Chicago, Illinois

The redevelopment of Cabrini-Green in Chicago is part of one of the most ambitious plans in the nation to redevelop existing failed public housing sites with lower-density mixed-income communities. Through good design and their location near downtown Chicago, the market-rate units in the development have commanded high prices while being located proximate to units reserved for low- and moderate-income households.

General Description

Cabrini-Green Homes, one of the nation's notorious public housing projects, and the neighborhood surrounding it, located in Chicago's urban core, have long been a pocket of poverty and crime. Cabrini-Green was particularly high profile because it was situated alongside affluent residential neighborhoods such as the Gold Coast and Lincoln Park as well as high-priced shopping along Michigan Avenue. The prime location for prospective market-rate buyers combined with growing pressure to solve the serious problems in the existing public housing has made it a desirable spot for redevelopment over the last decade.

CABRINI-GREEN HOMES/NEAR NORTH REDEVELOPMENT INITIATIVE FACTS

Land Use: An ambitious, large-scale public/private partnership approach to the redevelopment of Chicago's Cabrini-Green Homes, a mid–20th century public housing project, and the surrounding Near North neighborhood. The initiative aims to realize the privately developed construction of 2,150 units of new, mixed-income rental and for-sale housing in the form of rowhouses, duplexes, and mid-rise buildings. Public improvements include a new town center, a commercial district with a grocery store and shopping facilities, a district police station, new schools, a library, and a community center.

Affordability: All new developments on Chicago Housing Authority (CHA)—owned or city-owned land within the Near North Redevelopment Initiative (NNRI) area are required to include 50 percent market-rate units, 20 percent affordable housing units (i.e., those set aside for households earning less than 120 percent of the area median income [AMI] for for-sale units; below 80 percent AMI for rental units), and 30 percent CHA/public housing units (i.e., those reserved for households making below 80 percent of AMI).

Developments on land in the NNRI area that is not owned by the city or the CHA may have other income mixes, with leverage for negotiation provided through incentives such as access to area tax increment financing (TIF) funds.

FUNDING/PROGRAMS

Funding: HOPE VI, Near North Tax Increment Financing District, Low Income Housing Tax Credits, HOME/Community Development Block Grant (CDBG) loans, State of Illinois Affordable Housing Tax Credits, and private investment.

Programs: Near North Redevelopment Initiative, Cabrini-Green Consent Decree, and CHA Plan for Transformation.

Public Agencies/Departments: The City of Chicago Departments of Planning and Housing, Chicago Housing Authority, Illinois Housing Development Authority, and Federal Home Loan Bank.

Developers: MCL Companies, Holsten Real Estate Development Corp., Kenard Corp., Kimball Hill, Renaissance Realty Group, and Centrum Properties/Enterprise.

Architects: Roy Kruse & Associates, Smith & Smith, PappaGeorge Haymes, Bauhs Dring Main, and Fitzgerald & Associates.

Cabrini-Green Homes is being redeveloped as several lower-density, mixed-income neighborhoods incorporating new urbanist design. Located about a mile north of downtown on Chicago's Near North Side, the Cabrini-Green Homes were the physical manifestation of failed public housing policies that frequently isolated the poor in very high-density housing. The new master plan that will transform the community was selected as one of the five best architectural projects of the millennium by the *Wall Street Journal* and has been recognized by the American Institute of Architects for its high-quality design.

Named after Saint Frances Cabrini and 20th-century America labor leader William Green, the complex was constructed in four phases between 1942 and 1962: the 55 low-rise Frances Cabrini Rowhouses; 15 high rises in Cabrini Extension North and Cabrini Extension South; and eight buildings in the William Green Homes. At its peak, Cabrini-Green contained about 3,500 housing units and 15,000 residents covering 70 acres. Today, approximately 4,700 residents remain at Cabrini-Green Homes.

The redevelopment of Cabrini-Green and the surrounding Near North neighborhood is guided by several programs and agreements that have emerged in the last ten years:

■ $50 million in federal HOPE VI funding, awarded in 1994 to redevelop Cabrini Extension North and augmented by a HOPE VI Revitalization Plan in 1997;

■ the Near North Redevelopment Initiative (NNRI), a neighborhood plan adopted by the city in 1996;

■ the city's Near North TIF district, established at the same time as the NNRI to fund local public improvements;

■ the Cabrini-Green Consent Decree, a 2000 federal court settlement from a lawsuit filed by Cabrini-Green residents who feared that the expansive redevelopment would exclude them from the development process and displace them from their homes; and

■ the Chicago Housing Authority's 2000 Plan for Transformation, a comprehensive effort to reinvent all of the city's public housing and improve its appearance, quality, and culture.

The CHA and the city are working with private real estate developers to develop new communities that include a mix of market-rate, affordable, and public housing units. While the declining high-rise towers of Cabrini Extension North are being torn down, new development in the greater NNRI area consists of low- to mid-rise townhomes, condominiums, apartments, and single-family homes. However, as this ambitious undertaking reduces the total number of living units in the neighborhood, it is also decreasing the number of available public housing units. When the buildout for the NNRI area is complete, at least 700 new public housing units will replace 1,324 demolished original units. Approximately 60 percent of the units being demolished in the CHA's high-rise buildings were vacant when the plan began.

Yet, in exchange, the redevelopment creates mixed-income communities that provide housing opportunities for moderate-income families, market-rate buyers, and low-income households and offers social services such as child care and employment training to residents who need them. The intention is to create a physically and economically integrated community that provides not only a safer and more stable place to live, but also opportunities for low-income households to eventually break the cycle of poverty that was the hallmark of failed public housing policies of the past.

Development Process

Each mixed-income community developer in the Near North redevelopment area is selected by either the city of Chicago (when city land is a part of the redevelopment) or the CHA (when CHA land is being used) through a competitive procurement process in conjunction with a working group. The following steps are required of each new development to be constructed on land owned by the city or CHA, and thus under the jurisdiction of the Consent Decree.

CREATE A WORKING GROUP

The creation of a working group is the first step in the redevelopment process. A working group typically includes representatives of resident leadership, CHA staff, community partners, the Habitat Company (the Gautreaux Court–appointed receiver for development of new, nonelderly CHA housing), the Gautreaux Plaintiffs' Counsel, and the city of Chicago. A working group currently exists for each of the major mixed-income communities.

STRUCTURE FINANCING

Each project has a variety of sources of financial support. Typically, CHA funds are supplemented by private and public resources such as HOPE VI awards, tax credits, private mortgages, and tax-exempt bonds.

SELECT TENANTS AND NEGOTIATE LEASES

Applicants at each mixed-income development who are interested in renting market-rate, affordable, or public housing units are subject to site-specific leases and selection criteria drafted by the CHA and developer.

CLOSE BUILDINGS AND SCHEDULE DEMOLITION

The existing CHA-owned and -occupied buildings usually must be closed and demolished before construction can begin on a site. The CHA seeks to educate residents about their temporary and permanent housing options before closing a building. However, there are ongoing struggles between residents concerned about displacement and the CHA seeking to move ahead with redevelopment plans.

RENEW INFRASTRUCTURE

Once detailed redevelopment plans are in place, the CHA collaborates with a variety of city of Chicago departments, agencies, and utility companies to establish plans for new or upgraded infrastructure and public facilities. The infrastructure improvements typically include renewal of steam lines, upgrades to sewer lines, new or expanded public parks, public schools, police stations, as well as the reincorporation of formerly closed streets back into the Chicago street grid.

CLOSE THE REAL ESTATE TRANSACTION

With financing for redevelopment in place, the CHA and developer can close the real estate transaction. The closing indicates that HUD has approved the legal documents and the financial papers and planning documents are complete. It is only after the closing that construction can begin.

CONSTRUCTION AND MOVE-IN

Typically, the construction process takes 18 to 24 months from the date of the real estate transaction closing until the first unit is transferred to the CHA. Once units are transferred, residents can begin to move in.

Financing and Programs

A series of programs, funding, and lawsuits have shaped the redevelopment of Cabrini-Green over the last decade. They are presented below in chronological order.

HOPE VI (1994)

In 1994, Cabrini-Green became the first HOPE VI site in Chicago, receiving $50 million in HOPE VI Urban Revitalization Demonstration funds to redevelop the 18.4-acre Cabrini Extension North portion of the site. The final HOPE VI revitalization plan was adopted in 1997. (In 2002–2003, an additional $19 million in HOPE VI Public Housing Development funds was awarded for the demolition of Cabrini Extension South and the William Green Homes.)

In 1995, shortly after the HOPE VI plan was funded, the CHA was placed in federal receivership under the U.S. Department of Housing and Urban Development (HUD), at which time two Cabrini Extension buildings containing 398 units were demolished and no replacement units were provided. In 1999, HUD returned the CHA to local control.

NEAR NORTH REDEVELOPMENT INITIATIVE (1996)

In 1996, the city and CHA collaborated to produce the Near North Redevelopment Initiative (NNRI) and corresponding tax increment financing. The NNRI is the city of Chicago's master plan for Cabrini-Green and the surrounding neighborhood, covering 330 acres and bordered by North Avenue to the north, Halsted Street to the west, Chicago Avenue to the south, and Wells Street to the east. This plan expanded the HOPE VI Planning Area to coincide with the NNRI boundaries.

The redevelopment of the area, to be implemented by private developers, includes "on-site" projects located on CHA- or city-owned land, as well as "off-site" projects on land adjacent to or in the vicinity of the CHA land.

The NNRI is an effort to create a new, lower-density mixed-income community in the neighborhood, attract market-rate buyers, and move public housing residents out of high rises and into low-rise townhouses and flats. As an incentive, the CHA and the city provide the land formerly occupied by the Cabrini-Green projects and assist with securing development funds.

NEAR NORTH TAX INCREMENT FINANCING DISTRICT (1996)

At the same time the NNRI was established, a 23-year TIF district was established to support the redevelopment of Cabrini-Green (with boundaries nearly the same as those for the NNRI, with the exclusion of industrial property west of the Chicago River) with an estimated redevelopment budget of $281 million.

The revenues from the TIF bonds have been invested in public infrastructure, such as new roads, new sewer and drainage systems, public park expansion, a library, and the construction of new schools. The money raised from the TIF is also used as gap financing between the market price for a unit and the funding that the CHA has available to purchase the unit for public housing.

TENANTS' LAWSUIT (1996) AND THE CABRINI-GREEN CONSENT DECREE (2000)

Residents of Cabrini-Green were incensed with the new plan: the NNRI not only nullified the previous development agreement with the local advisory council (LAC), but also sought to demolish additional buildings and permanently relocate more public housing residents off site. In October 1996, the Cabrini LAC filed a lawsuit against both the city and the CHA, claiming that the NNRI would discriminate against African Americans, women, and children by substantially reducing the number of public housing units in the neighborhood, displacing residents who wanted to stay, and proceeding with demolition before replacement housing was available. In addition, the court case charged that Cabrini residents had been excluded from the planning process in violation of federal law. The lawsuit halted the site's redevelopment until the conflict was finally resolved in 2000, with a federal Consent Decree settlement.

Under the 2000 Consent Decree, the parcel of Cabrini-Green known as Extension North must include coordination among public housing residents, the CHA, the city of Chicago, and private developers. The decree allowed for the demolition of six Cabrini high rises and expanded the HOPE VI planning area to be defined by the boundaries of the TIF rather than by only the public housing site. The agreement called for the construction of 2,150 mixed-income housing units throughout the TIF area: 1,050 market-rate homes, 270 affordable homes, and 700 public housing units in a 50-20-30 income mix.

The settlement also established the criteria that must be fulfilled before the three occupied high rises could be demolished and allowed the Cabrini-Green LAC to have up to a 50 percent ownership share in the entity chosen to be the developer of the new housing, with the final share to be determined by the developers in their bids.

With the accepted Consent Decree settlement, the CHA started redevelopment efforts in 2001.

New units on publicly owned land are required to include 50 percent market-rate units, 20 percent affordable housing units, and 30 percent CHA/public housing units. Shown below are the Renaissance North Apartments, which include units for residents with a mix of incomes.

CHA PLAN FOR TRANSFORMATION (2000)

In 2000, the Chicago Housing Authority unveiled its "Plan for Transformation," an ambitious plan to redevelop public housing throughout Chicago that seeks to renew the physical structure of CHA properties, promote self-sufficiency for public housing residents, and reform administration of the CHA. The goal of the redevelopment efforts is to build or rehabilitate approximately 25,000 units of housing by the end of 2009, including about 6,100 family units to be redeveloped as new mixed-income housing. The CHA's overarching goal is to physically reintegrate the residents into the fabric of the surrounding community to end the years of isolation.

In addition, the city's department of housing (DOH) and the Illinois Housing Development Authority (IHDA) have contributed significant funds to the Plan for Transformation. DOH has committed half of its affordable, multifamily housing resources over ten years to the Plan for Transformation. These resources, including Low Income Housing Tax Credits (LIHTCs) and HOME/CDBG loans, and tax-exempt bonds have been and will continue to be used extensively in the Cabrini redevelopment. The DOH commitment equals roughly $2.6 million in LIHTCs and $17 million in loan funds per year for ten years. The IHDA has committed $3 million per year in LIHTCs to the Plan

for Transformation. Both DOH and IHDA provided LIHTCs and loan funds for North Town Village and DOH provided a HOME Loan, tax-exempt bond financing, and bond-generated tax credits to Renaissance North.

Planning and Design

The overall design for developments in the NNRI area was established via a two-day charrette with the working group for the city of Chicago. The plan sought to create a unified strategy and design guidelines incorporating new urbanist principles for the multiphase development of new mixed-income housing, public schools and parks, and a commercial center as well the reestablishment of the former street grid from the 1940s that had been obliterated in the public housing "superblocks."

Beyond these initial guidelines, the CHA does not have specific design standards that apply to the new construction, and typically developers design according to a market-rate standard. The developments incorporate con-

(Above) The reduced residential density at Old Town Square contributes to more green space.

(Left) Units at Old Town Square typically have oak floors, fireplaces, patios, and yards. The exterior design complements the character of the surrounding neighborhood.

temporary townhouse or lower-density architecture that complements the character of the surrounding neighborhood. Amenities in the units include oak floors, real fireplaces, patios, and yards.

The CHA works with the development team when designing the buildings to determine the current bedroom needs for public housing families. The market-rate, affordable,

(Above) Orchard Park reestablishes the former street grid from the 1940s that had been obliterated by the public housing "superblocks."

(Below) Privately developed mixed-income rowhouses, duplexes, and mid-rise buildings, like these at Orchard Park in the Near North neighborhood, are all part of the new construction that is replacing the Cabrini-Green Homes high-rise public housing.

and CHA rental units are indistinguishable, although buyers of the for-sale market-rate units may purchase upgrades. However, the design of the new construction does seek to meet three overarching criteria:

- reintegrate the public housing residents into the fabric of the city;

- provide ample open space; and

- create a safe and secure environment.

To achieve the desired level of safety, the CHA and the city of Chicago have retained the services of an architectural design consultant with expertise in designing for security. This security design consultant reviews each of the designs and makes recommendations such as how to improve lighting or fencing or create more open areas to assist with policing.

Affordability and Management/Marketing

AFFORDABILITY

New housing developed on land owned by the CHA or the city of Chicago within the NNRI area must contain a 50-20-30 mix, by the terms of the Consent Decree: 50 percent market-rate housing, 20 percent affordable housing (80 to 120 percent of the AMI for for-sale housing; under 80 percent of the AMI for rental housing), and 30 percent public housing (below 80 percent of the AMI). For each of these developments, the developer typically is required to comply with tax credit/HOME-funded unit affordability standards for 30 years; CHA units must meet public housing affordability standards for 40 years.

The Consent Decree additionally specified:

- Half of the 700 public housing units are reserved for families with at least one employed household member; the other half have no work requirement.

- There shall be at least 270 affordable rental units; all are reserved for households with at least one working member.

- Some portion of any affordable for-sale units shall be available to families earning 60 percent of the AMI or less.

- Density shall be no more than 49 dwelling units per acre.

Other housing developments on privately acquired property may have a mix of incomes, but on terms negotiated between the developer and the city or CHA.

MANAGEMENT

Developers have hired private property management firms to manage the rental property being developed. The property management firms maintain the units and conduct the screening process.

Each developer of city- and CHA-owned land must incorporate the provision of community and supportive services into the project, including job training and employment opportunities. Some $8 million of the HOPE VI funds were dedicated for providing such services, and only Cabrini-Green Extension residents are eligible for the use of these funds. However, money raised by the TIF allocation may be used more broadly for low-income residents in the TIF district.

For example, at North Town Village (NTV), relocated families moving in from Cabrini-Green Extension receive a full-service needs assessment. Residents in need of social services can get help with case management. Local churches and other service providers are contracted to help NTV residents handle drug abuse, home maintenance, financial planning, domestic violence counseling, and other issues. NTV also coordinates with the New City YMCA's Local Economic and Employment Development Council to provide employment training, adult education, child care, and transportation.

PROJECTS TO DATE

Units located on Cabrini-Green land are considered "on site," while "off-site" developments are located on other land owned by the city or CHA. Full buildout is anticipated by 2010.

Note: some of the developments described below are in the Near North Redevelopment Area and predate the Consent Decree, but were built on city- or CHA-owned land and contain affordable and public housing units that count toward the required numbers.

MOHAWK NORTH (OFF SITE)

Date of Opening: 1996.

Units/Affordability: 92 units: for-sale townhomes, condominiums, and single-family homes, with the exception of 16 public housing rentals (20 percent), which are leased to the CHA on a 40-year lease.

Developer: MCL Companies.

Architect: Roy Kruse & Associates.

Price Range: Initially sold for $124,900 to $452,900. Mohawk Partners/Infill (off site).

Date of Opening: 2000.

15 units: five market-rate for sale, five affordable for sale, and five CHA.

Developers: Smith & Smith and Monterrey.

Architect: Smith & Smith.

Price Range: Initially sold for $199,900 to $370,000. Old Town Square (off site).

Date of Opening: 1998.

Units/Affordability: 113 units: for-sale condominiums, townhouses, and single-family homes, with the exception of 16 public housing rental units, which are leased to the CHA on a 40-year lease.

Developer: MCL Companies.

Architect: PappaGeorge Haymes.

Price Range: Initially sold for $125,000 to $327,000.

NORTH TOWN VILLAGE (OFF SITE)

Date of Opening: 1998.

Units/Affordability: 261 units: rental and for-sale townhomes, duplexes, and condominiums.

Rental: 79 CHA units, 39 affordable housing, 37 market-rate, and one janitor's unit.

For-sale: 105 market-rate units.

Developers: Holsten Real Estate Development Corp. and Kenard Corp.

Architect: Bauhs Dring Main.

Price Range: From $119,000 to $400,000; rents, from $367 to $1,400.

OLD TOWN VILLAGE EAST AND WEST (OFF SITE)

Date of Opening: 2003.

Units/Affordability: 273 units: for-sale single-family homes, condominiums, and townhomes, with the exception of 66 public housing rental units, which are leased to the CHA on a 40-year lease.

Developer: MCL Companies.

Architect: Peter Holsten.

Price Range: From $265,000 to $850,000.

VILLAGE NORTH (ON SITE)

Date of Opening: Will open in two phases, with the first phase opening in 2006–2007.

Units/Affordability: 680 units, condominiums, and townhomes, both rental and for sale. Exact unit mix to be determined.

Developers: Holsten Real Estate Development Corp., Kimball Hill, and Cabrini New Beginnings.

Architect: Fitzgerald & Associates.

Price Range: To be determined.

RENAISSANCE NORTH (OFF SITE)

Date of Opening: 2003.

Units/Affordability: 59 rental units: 29 market-rate units, 18 public housing units, and 12 affordable units for 60 percent or less of AMI.

Developer: RRG Development, Inc.

Architect: Roy H. Kruse and Associates, Ltd.

Property Management: Renaissance Realty Group, Inc., Management Division.

Rent Range: $350 to $2,050 per month.

ORCHARD PARK TOWNHOMES (OFF SITE)

Date of Opening: 2000.

Units/Affordability: 46 townhouse units, with 13 public housing units.

Architect: PappaGeorge Haymes.

Developers: Chicago Dwellings Association and the CHA.

Price Range: Initially sold for $175,000 to $225,000.

DOMAIN LOFTS (OFF SITE)

Date of Opening: 2003.

Units/Affordability: 16 CHA units in a larger for-sale condominium development.

Developer: Centrum Properties.

Price Range: Initially sold for $200,000 to $500,000.

Lessons Learned

■ Balance design considerations with cost control. Certain design features—such as the masonry exterior of many of the properties—while consistent with the desired character for the neighborhood, were extremely expensive and raised the cost of the developments considerably.

■ Plan for outdoor spaces. Anticipate the need for play spaces for children. Take advantage of the reduced residential density to create more green space and make it possible for children to play outside and be supervised by their parents in proximity to their homes.

■ Consider affordable homeownership programs. Provide public housing residents the opportunity to buy homes in new developments.

■ Incorporate a group effort in the process. Including neighborhood residents, public housing residents, CHA staff, department of planning staff, department of housing staff, etc., throughout the planning and development process is essential to the success of a project.

■ Recognize the reality of market-rate prices. When predicting project costs and revenue, recognize that market-rate properties in a mixed-income project may be somewhat depressed compared with all-market-rate projects. However, in strong real estate market areas like that of Cabrini-Green, developers have been able to raise their prices during initial marketing.

■ Review the budget carefully. The total development costs allowed under HOPE VI do not cover the actual development costs of the project. As a result, TIF money is being used to supplement the acquisition of CHA units.

■ Address the fact that lowering density reduces the number of housing units. When density goes down and mixed-income communities replace exclusively low-income neighborhoods, agencies need to consider the impact of a reduced number of available public housing units.

Endnotes

1 Joint Center for Housing Studies of Harvard University, *The State of the Nation's Housing 2004* (Cambridge, MA; President and Fellows of Harvard College, 2004, p.15).

2 United States Department of Housing and Urban Development, *Unequal Burden: Income and Racial Disparities in Subprime Lending in America* (http://www.hud.gov/library/bookshelf18/pressrel/subprime.html).

3 Center for Housing Policy/National Housing Conference, *America's Working Families and the Housing Landscape, 1997–2001* (Washington, D.C., National Housing Conference, 2002, p.7).

4 Joint Center, *the State of the Nation's Housing*, p. 25.

5 Center for Housing Policy/National Housing Conference, *Paycheck to Paycheck: Working Families and the Cost of Housing in America* (Washington, D.C., National Housing Conference, 2001, p. 25).

6 Joint Center, *the State of the Nation's Housing*, p. 28.

7 Green building refers to commercial and residential real estate development that meets numerous environmental standards for energy efficiency, thoughtful use of resources, recycling of waste products, etc. The LEED (Leadership in Energy and Environmental Design) Green Building Rating System is a voluntary consensus-based national standard for high-performance sustainable buildings. LEED standards are set by members of the U.S. Green Building Council. More information can be found at www.usgbc.org.

8 David Schrank and Tim Lomax, *The 2005 Urban Mobility Report (College Station, TX: Texas Transportation Institute, the Texas A&M University System, May 2005).*

9 Community Action Network, Urgent Issues Action Plan, Affordable Housing, http://www.caction.org/IssueAreas/UrgentIssues/Housing.htm.

10 Annys Shin, "2005 Real Estate Annual Housing Outlook—Montgomery County," *Washington Post,* 23 March, 2005, p. H07.

11 http://quickfacts.census.gov/qfd/states/24/24031.html.

12 http://www.capitalbay.com/teacherssalary.asp.

13 David Schrank and Tim Lomax, *The 2005 Urban Mobility Report (College Station, TX: Texas Transportation Institute, the Texas A&M University System, May 2005).*

14 American Affordable Housing Institute, Department of Urban Studies and Community Health of Bloustein School of Planning and Public Policy. http://policy.rutgers.edu/eah/aahi.html.

15 The Chapter 40B Task Force, "Chapter 40B Task Force: Findings and Recommendations, Report to Governor Mitt Romney." available at www.state.ma.us/dhcd/Ch40Btf.

16 Governor Mitt Romney, "Fixing it First in Massachusetts," *Housing Facts and Findings,* vol. 6, issue 1.

17 Green building refers to commercial and residential real estate development that meets numerous environmental standards for energy efficiency, thoughtful use of resources, recycling of waste products, etc. The LEED (Leadership in Energy and Environmental Design) Green Building Rating System is a voluntary consensus-based national standard for high-performance sustainable buildings. LEED standards are set by members of the U.S. Green Building Council. More information can be found at www.usgbc.org.

18 Whorisky, Peter. "Find the Affordable Housing in this Picture." *Washington Post.*